LEARNING
FROM CHINA

THE TAO OF
THE CITY

CARL FINGERHUTH

LEARNING FROM CHINA

THE TAO OF THE CITY

BIRKHÄUSER – PUBLISHERS FOR ARCHITECTURE

BASEL · BOSTON · BERLIN

Self-portrait, M.C. Escher

———

LABORING IN PHILOSOPHY, MUCH LIKE LABORING IN ARCHI-
TECTURE, IS IN FACT WORK ON ONESELF. ON ONE'S OWN ATTITUDES.
ON HOW ONE PERCEIVES THINGS. (AND WHAT ONE DEMANDS OF
THINGS.)

—— *Ludwig Wittgenstein*

FOREWORD

This book deals with caring for the gestalt of our cities through the art, science, and philosophy of what I call urbanism. Cultures reveal their identities and aspirations through the gestalt of their cities. Thus, urban images reflect the social, economic, and cultural consciousness of a city's inhabitants. These images are preserved in the gestalt of the city like geological stratum. As a culture's consciousness evolves, new energy develops and must become incorporated into the city's gestalt to ensure its existence as a city of its time. Carefully integrating these transformations is the primary task of urbanism.

In order to discuss caring for the gestalt of our cities, for the urbanism of our time, I must first define the specific situation we find ourselves in today. Based on my own experiences dealing with urban transformation, I describe the current age as the beyond-the-modern era.

In many ways, this book is anchored in my own personal experiences and has become, in the spirit of Wittgenstein, a veritable work on myself. It is my personal view of things and I make no claims at absolute truth. Still, I will draw from the works of many who have already explored our transformation from modernism: Jean Gebser, Carl Gustav Jung, Hans Küng, Ken Wilber, Rupert Sheldrake, and many others. To date, however, few have drawn correlations to the gestalt of our cities.

It is my belief that our dealings with cities were intensely limited by the one-dimensionality of modern ideals. A deep-seated fear of emotion and spirituality, coupled with a craving for control fueled by devotion to the rigid doctrines of science and technology, created a modernism characterized by severely reduced consciousness. This resulted in cities that were aggressive, impoverished, and depressingly banal. Our times call for a greater consciousness, one that allows for what the Taoists refer to as "the world of the ten thousand things." This new awareness could lead to a far more meaningful approach to caring for our cities. It could also lead to better and more beautiful cities.

Reintegrating the ideals that modernism helped stunt and suppress, and reconnecting those through art, science, and philosophy, is a crucial step toward fostering urban change. To this end, we must accept and integrate the principal themes of beyond-the-modern consciousness. There are four primary points to consider:

– Reintegrating the non-rational dimension of human existence;
– Reintegrating consciousness of the polarity of all existence;
– Reintegrating consciousness of man's unity with nature;
– Reintegrating the essence of aesthetics.

We can, and should, preserve fundamental aspects of modernism. This book isn't about overthrowing the dogma of modern urbanism. It is about striving to integrate what is radically new into how we deal with our constantly evolving cities. Our times are rich with change and our cities constantly morphing. I believe it is time to address the subject.

Venice, illustration from Marco Polo's travel
diary *Il Milione*

———

KUBLAI KHAN DOES NOT NECESSARILY BELIEVE IN EVERYTHING
MARCO POLO SAYS WHEN HE DESCRIBES THE CITIES VISITED
ON HIS EXPEDITION, BUT THE EMPEROR OF THE TARTARS DOES
CONTINUE LISTENING TO THE YOUNG VENETIAN WITH GREATER
ATTENTION AND CURIOSITY THAN HE SHOWS ANY OTHER MESSEN-
GER OR EXPLORER OF HIS... AND POLO SAID: "THE INFERNO OF
THE LIVING IS NOT SOMETHING THAT WILL BE; IF THERE IS ONE,
IT IS WHAT IS ALREADY HERE, THE INFERNO WHERE WE LIVE EVERY
DAY, THAT WE FORM BY BEING TOGETHER. THERE ARE TWO WAYS
TO ESCAPE SUFFERING IT. THE FIRST IS EASY FOR MANY: ACCEPT
THE INFERNO AND BECOME SUCH A PART OF IT THAT YOU CAN
NO LONGER SEE IT. THE SECOND IS RISKY AND DEMANDS CONSTANT
VIGILANCE AND APPREHENSION: SEEK AND LEARN TO RECOGNIZE
WHO AND WHAT, IN THE MIDST OF THE INFERNO, ARE NOT INFERNO,
THEN MAKE THEM ENDURE, GIVE THEM SPACE."

—— *Italo Calvino* [1]

01

THE GAME OF THE CITY

GIVING THE CITY
ENDURANCE AND SPACE

In the magical lore of central Switzerland's mountain farmers, there is a tale about a herd of cows that suddenly disappeared into thin air during the annual cattle drive from Alpine pastures. The farmer knew to "*nit derglychä z'tuä*," a Swiss-German expression that roughly translates into: "pretend nothing happened." Based on his cultural traditions, he knew that such conflicting realities were best disregarded. The wisest response to this sort of situation was for him to ignore the missing cows and keep walking down the path, cracking his whip and whistling as though all were well. Clearly, should he do so, the herd would pop back into his reality a few hundred meters down the path to the valley. [2] Such magical tales of the *outre monde*, frequently told by wise women and shamans, underscored the belief that while a parallel world indeed exists beyond the reality of daily life, one had best ignore it. It is best, in other words, to pretend nothing happened.

Our approach to dealing with the contemporary world is very similar. There is a profound discrepancy between the perceived modern world, where our existence and activities are dominated by rationality, and our individual intuitive sense of reality. As confirmed by the many fundamentally new insights emerging across multiple fields of study, we intuit that there is a larger, more complex world beyond that of daily routine and rational consciousness. Yet within mainstream thinking, and in our dealings with cities, intuition is rarely taken seriously. Like the cowherd, we prefer to play it safe and pretend nothing happened. Thus everything remains as it was.

This book presents an account of the city beyond modern time. It looks at how we can begin to integrate our intuitive knowledge into transforming the world. At issue is not merely the practice of transformation but also that which lies behind it. Aristotle defined it as the theory and poetry of the city: It is "neither a theoretical (such as geometry) nor practical (such as politics) science, but rather a knowledge of design and creation" [3]. I intend to demonstrate how an intuitive understanding of the beyond-the-modern world can influence how we design and create the forms and structures of our contemporary cities.

Your and my age and the age of the world, by Anselm Kiefer

THE CITY AS VISIBLE MYTH

Our collective social, economic, and cultural
will create the gestalt of our cities. It is
through banding together that we become
able to give a place cohesive structure and
form. As such, the spaces we create are partially determined by physical needs – roofs for
protection against rain and snow, fences and
walls for protection against wild beasts and
strangers, sewers to prevent contaminating
clean water. But a city's gestalt also springs
from the interweaving of our existential needs
with the emotional and spiritual expressions
of our humanity. Today, this expression has
been buried.

Our physical needs, desires, and emotional
and spiritual longings are all reflected within
our cities. In *Invisible Cities*, Italo Calvino
describes fifty-five cities through the mythical
depictions of some of the most basic aspects
of our human existence. He deals with
concepts such as memory, desire, symbol,
exchange, and name. I have chosen three of
these concepts as a point of departure for
this account.

THE CITY AND MEMORY

"Leaving there and proceeding for three days toward the east, you reach Diomira, a city with sixty silver domes, bronze statues of all the gods, streets paved with lead, a crystal theatre, a golden cock that crows each morning on a tower. All these beauties will already be familiar to the visitor, who has seen them also in other cities. But the special quality of this city for the man who arrives there on a September evening, when the days are growing shorter and the multicolored lamps are lighted all at once at the doors of the food stalls and from a terrace a woman's voice cries ooh!, is that he feels envy toward those who now believe they have once before lived an evening identical to this and who think they were happy, that time."[4]

THE CITY AND DESIRE

"In the center of Fedora, that gray stone metropolis, stands a metal building with a crystal globe in every room. Looking into each globe, you see a blue city, the model of a different Fedora. These are the forms the city could have taken if, for one reason or another, it had not become what we see today. In every age someone, looking at Fedora as it was, imagined a way of making it the ideal city, but while he constructed his miniature model, Fedora was already no longer the same as before, and what had been until yesterday a possible future became only a toy in a glass globe."[5]

THE CITY AND EYES

"When you have forded the river, when you have crossed the mountain pass, you suddenly find before you the city of Moriana, its alabaster gates transparent in the sunlight, its coral columns supporting pediments encrusted with serpentine, its villas all of glass like aquariums where the shadows of dancing girls with silvery scales swim beneath the medusa-shaped chandeliers. If this is not your first journey, you already know that cities like this have an obverse: you have only to walk in a semicircle and you will come into view of Moriana's hidden face, an expanse of rusting sheet metal, sackcloth, planks bristling with spikes, pipes black with soot, piles of tins, blind walls with fading signs, frames of staved-in straw chairs, ropes good only for hanging oneself from a rotten beam."[6]

All these themes are contained for each of us within the actual gestalt of our cities. Thus, cities such as Las Vegas, Santorini, Chernobyl, New York, Venice, Como, Mahabalipuram, or Marrakesh, represent much more to me than simply names on a map. Their gestalts – the aspects which, as Calvino wrote, "endure, give them space" – tell many a magical tale. Their symbols contain archetypal meaning; their spaces allow me to dream, celebrate, or grieve.

The City as Stage Set

I remember thousands of colorful lights
one evening in Las Vegas. A boxing match
was to take place at Caesar's Palace between
Mohammed Ali and another great hero. Two
burly policemen stood by their sparkling
Harley Davidson motorcycles in a bright pool
of light at an intersection in front of the
hotel. Carefully avoiding the litter of countless
empty beer cans, the two coolly directed the
flow of thousands of glittering limousines
arriving for the fight.

The City as Dream

I remember a pitch-black nighttime ferry
ride across the Aegean Sea. In the dark skies
above, a wreath of lights suddenly appeared
out of nowhere, like a mystical crown in
the firmament. Half an hour later, we dropped
anchor in Santorini harbor. Upon climbing
the path into town, it became clear that our
so-called spiritual apparition was in fact a
bustling Dionysian temple. In bright daylight,
Santorini transformed into a purely physical
city, with pale Northerners in shorts, domed
houses converted into souvenir shops, and
ads for Coca-Cola.

The City as Catastrophe of Human Hubris

I remember my profound fear upon hearing the news of the fire at the nuclear reactor in Chernobyl and how I experienced the same feeling once again a few months later. Thousands of tons of chemicals were burning in a warehouse fire on the edge of Basel, the Swiss city in which I lived. In the middle of the night, police cars drove through the city with loudspeakers warning residents not to leave their homes, to keep their windows tightly shut, and to listen to the radio for news about the toxic cloud.

The City as Path Through the World

I remember experiencing the sheer mass and variety of New York City during a marathon through its five boroughs: Across the Staten Island bridge to Brooklyn, through Queens and then across the Queensboro bridge to Manhattan, running up First Avenue to the Bronx, crossing over to Harlem, and finally down Fifth Avenue and into Central Park.

The City as Labyrinth

I remember my fascination with the mystery of the city when, at age twelve, I played David Livingstone exploring the African jungle and set out to search for the route from the Piazza San Marco to the statue of Bartolomeo Colleoni. Venice was the labyrinth of the Minotaur and my task as a modern-day explorer, clutching a city map, was to find my way to the monster and back again in one piece.

The City as Palimpsest

I remember walking through Como and witnessing a hodgepodge of two thousand years of urban transformation. The city's very first incarnation was as a Celtic port. Then came the austere structure of a Roman city, followed by a labyrinthine conversion into a medieval city. This would become overlaid first by a copy of Paris' Rue Rivoli, and finally, by an effort to redefine the city's center through the poignant presence of the Casa Del Fascio, the hub of fascist government. A story rewritten many, many times.

The City as Magical Place

I remember an encounter with thirty massive white buffalo near Mahabalipuram on the shores of the Indian Ocean. They seemed part of another world. I believe I was truly momentarily transported into an alternate reality. The doctor spoke of amnesia and prescribed aspirin and I came back into my everyday reality.

The City as Magician's Stage

I remember an oasis of fire in the midst of a dark night. It was in the city of Marrakesh, at the foot of the Atlas Mountains. Dervishes, soothsayers, acrobats, snake-charmers, and spice and amulet venders were staging an intoxicating spectacle of dance, music, and magical tricks on the central square of Djemaa el-Fna, which in Arabic means "Gathering of the Executed."

SOCIETY	BUILDING	SPACE
Needs	Regional planning	Plot
Goals	Urban design	Neighborhood
Values	Architecture	City

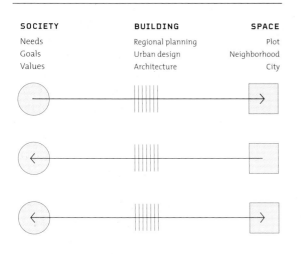

The city evolves out of the constant interaction between society and space.

THE CITY AS THE WAY WE WANT TO BE

The left-hand column of this diagram refers to society. Humans feel, sense, think, and intuit. They want security, demand justice, and dream of eternal happiness and beauty. Each of these goals can be experienced on a spiritual, emotional, or physical plane. To live on the physical plane means to work with one's body, to take care of one's body, and to listen to one's body. To live on the emotional plane means to register feelings, to interpret them, and to react to them. To live on the spiritual plane means to seek, sense, and process intuitions of unity with the cosmos. Living can therefore be interpreted as dealing with needs, articulating goals, and integrating visions and dreams. This gives humankind its identity, its presence, and its gestalt.

The right-hand column refers to physical space. It deals with the *topos*, space as defined by its gestalt. It facilitates action or resists it. *Topos* creates needs or satisfies them, it is the hill, the narrows of the river, the conditions and resources of nature. But

topos is also the existing city whose streets, lots, and buildings have been created over the course of time.

Cities evolve out of the interaction between the left and right columns. Built of stone, metal, and glass, the physical city is a human artifact, a body created and nourished solely by and through people. Collective emotions and spiritual intuitions manifest themselves through it. It is through this interaction that cities receive identity, presence, and gestalt.

When Martin Heidegger describes the manner in which we humans are on earth dwelling, I believe he is expressing the same idea. "What, then, does *Bauen*, building, mean? The Old English and High German word for building, *buan*, means to dwell. This signifies: to remain, to stay in a place. The real meaning of the verb *bauen*, namely, to dwell, has been lost to us. But a covert trace of it has been preserved in the German word *Nachbar*, neighbor. The neighbor is in Old English the *neahgebur; neah*, near, and *gebur*, dweller. The Nachbar is the *nachgebur*, the *Nachgebauer*, the near-dweller, he who dwells nearby ... Where the word *bauen* still speaks in its original sense it also says *how far* the nature of dwelling reaches. That is, *bauen, buan, bhu, beo* are our word *bin* in the versions: *ich bin*, I am, *du bist*, you are, the imperative form *bis*, be. What then does *ich bin* mean? The old word *bauen*, to which the *bin* belongs, answers: *ich bin, du bist* meaning: I dwell, you dwell. The way in which you *are* and I am, the manner in which we humans are on earth, is *Buan*, dwelling." [7]

The city serves to protect the individual and help him evolve and flourish. It also serves society as a whole, as an agency of evolution, preservation, development, and progress. The city is constantly reborn through the actions of society, in a never-ending stream of individual and collective manifestations of human thought, feeling, perception, and intuition.

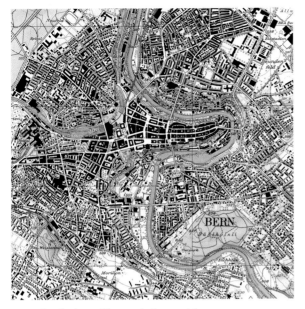

Berne: urban development from 1190 to the present day

Prague: urban development from the ninth century to
the present day

Urbanism is the manifestation, through art, science, and philosophy, of the continuous human drive to give cities gestalt. It is about transformation, about giving form and gestalt, and it is about enabling epiphanies. To put it bluntly, urbanism provides a service to society. It creates and imparts gestalt to societal needs, wishes, and dreams. Urbanism is therefore not simply theory, doctrine, or a set of scientific findings. It is a practice, and practice requires action.

In modernist terminology, urban design is connected with the act of building and it assumes that caring for a city's transformation primarily involves only that. Building is associated with newness and growth, and with the conversion of mineral matter. Yet the transformation of a city can also be about preserving existing elements, abstaining from doing something, or planting trees instead of assembling layers of stone. Urbanism therefore encompasses much more than the physical act of building cities. According to Martin Heidegger's interpretation, building is about how we desire to exist on earth. The gestalt of the city is an expression of our being. As an architect, when I am called upon to build, I must first inquire, listen, and be mindful of who I am building for, how they wish to live, and where they find themselves most at home.

If I choose to define building as the process of translating people's needs, values, and dreams into gestalt, then I may also define urbanism as the practice of caring for the transformation of cities. But if the definition of building is simply reduced to the act of constructing through the combination of materials or parts, then my subject matter becomes too narrow. I choose to use the term urbanism for lack of a better word since a handy term that evokes an expanded understanding of caring for the transformation of cities does not yet exist. Thus, a clear distinction must be made between urban design and urbanism – from the French word *urbanisme* – which I define as the science, art, and philosophy of caring for the transformation of the city. Urban design refers to the field of work that lies somewhere between the parameters of urban planning and architecture. Urbanism, on the other hand, encompasses all the disciplines involved in the transformation of the city. Spatially, those disciplines include architecture, urban design, urban planning, and regional planning. Applied disciplines include architecture, engineering, landscape- and traffic-planning. From this perspective, urbanism involves caring for the transformation of a city in all its complexity. It aligns the various disciplines and coordinates their activities. Urbanism taps into a hybrid, rhizoid network of existing spatial characteristics, of multiple layers of physical interventions in a space that was long ago shaped by large-scale plans, minimal corrections, and the occasional decision to abstain from action.

FOUR GAMES OF THE CITY

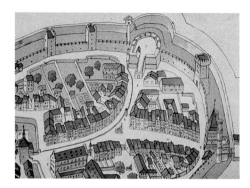

Basel's Spalenvorstadt as a link between the city gate built in 1200, and the city gate built in 1400, in a depiction of the city from 1615

Today's existing plan

A BUILDING GAP: SPALENVORSTADT 11 IN BASEL

In 1979, I became the city architect of Basel, a two-thousand-year-old Swiss city nestled on a bend of the Rhine river and bordering France and Germany. As such, I participated in the great game of the city on many levels. Precisely at that time, however, urbanism was caught in a state of paralysis. In the 1980s, new energies had emerged but not yet been allowed to develop. The city still identified strongly with modernism and remained inflexible toward beyond-the-modern ideas. The flux of images had come to a standstill and could not be implemented as gestalt within urbanism. To begin with, I had to lead the city out of this cultural blockade.

I had discovered a building gap owned by the city in the historical part of town. This created an opportunity to engage in a small-scale but intensive game with the city. I organized a competition open to all Swiss architects for the development of this open space, hoping to initiate public dialogue about architecture and urbanism within the city.

The intensity of gestalt is felt most strongly when the authors of a project are forced to face challenging conditions. To create a new building within the existing structure of a landmark-protected neighborhood was an unusual task at that time. Adding another level of complexity to the project, a tall underpass needed to be incorporated into the building to accommodate the municipal fire department. Lacking comparable situations from which to draw inspiration, competitors were forced to create and explore entirely new concepts and ideas.

Altogether, 137 proposals were submitted. It was fascinating to observe how many archetypal approaches were represented in the submissions. Within the community, and even the country, the project had much resonance. The building was completed three years later. The design, by Zurich-based architects Ueli Marbach and Arthur Rüegg, displayed an intensive aesthetic implementation of the themes of the time. With deep respect for the existing urban structure as well as for the formal elements of the site, the architects developed a subtle interplay between structure and form that strongly reflected the energies of the period.

The building gap on a lot occupied by the fire department

The new structure by architects Marbach and Rüegg, viewed from the street...

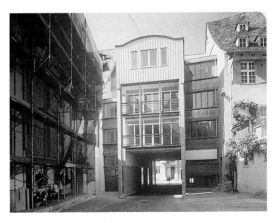

...and from the rear courtyard

DIE BAULÜCKE

UND
137
VORSCHLÄGE,
SIE
NACH
HUNDERT
JAHREN
WIEDER
ZU
SCHLIESSEN

NR 7   NR 9   NR 11   NR 13

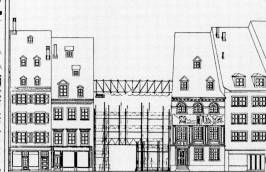

Die Gegenwart ist nicht dazu verflucht, die Geschichte nachäffen zu müssen. Denkmalschutz geht nicht über alles. Auch in historischer Umgebung darf wieder selbstbewusst gebaut werden. Es ist erlaubt, eine Idee zu haben.

Die Botschaft kommt aus Basel-Stadt. Dort fasste Carl Fingerhuth, Kantonsbaumeister seit drei Jahren, vorher Architekt und Planer in Zürich, einen schöpferischen Entschluss: Eine kleine Baulücke in einer Altstadtstrasse sei mit einem Neubau, der sich nicht alt zu geben brauche, zu schliessen. Das Baudepartement des Kantons schrieb darauf im Frühjahr 1981 einen gesamtschweizerischen Architekturwettbewerb aus, als «Beitrag zur europäischen Stadterneuerungskampagne 1981». Das gesamtschweizerische Interesse an dem Miniatur-Bauvorhaben übertraf alle Erwartungen: 304 Architekten aus dem ganzen Land bezogen die Wettbewerbsunterlagen; 137 reichten einen Vorschlag ein: ein nationales Festival der Baukunst am kleinstmöglichen Objekt.

Die Strasse mit der Baulücke im Besitz des Kantons heisst Spalenvorstadt und führt am westlichen Rand der Altstadt von der sogenannten Lyss zum Spalentor. Sie entstand wie das meiste des alten Ba-

Das mit dem 1. Preis ausgezeichnete Projekt von Franz Romero, Architekt ETH/ HTL, Zürich. Auf etwas biedere Art greift dieser Vorschlag auf Elemente des «Neuen Bauens» der dreissiger Jahre zurück. Romero erwähnt im Projektbericht ausdrücklich Professor O. R. Salvisberg als Paten (von Salvisberg in Zürich zum Beispiel das Geschäftshaus «Bleicherhof» am Bleicherweg, 1939/40). Der Entscheid des Preisgerichts für diesen Zwitter zwischen «historisierend» und «modern» muss als vorsichtig oder sogar ängstlich bezeichnet werden.

sel bald nach 1356, nach dem grossen Erdbeben. Manche Bauten an der Strasse sind im Lauf der Jahrhunderte mehrmals verändert, umgebaut, ersetzt worden. «Reines» Mittelalter stellt die Spalenvorstadt nicht vor. Wohl gehört das Ensemble zur Schutzzone; es gilt jedoch nicht als Denkmal erster Klasse.

Das Haus Spalenvorstadt 11 fehlt seit über hundert Jahren. Über die frühere Füllung der Lücke sind nur ungefähre Informationen archiviert. Alte Pläne oder Ansichten, die eine präzise historische Rekonstruktion zuliessen, existieren keine. Also: «Es soll gezeigt werden, dass Bauen in heutigen Formen und Materialien auch in einem historischen Ensemble möglich ist, wenn dem kulturellen Erbe der gebührende Respekt gezollt wird» (Bericht der Wettbewerbsjury). Die Zahnlücke wurde den Architekten zu beliebiger Füllung freigegeben. Weder Nutzung noch Bauhöhe waren vorgeschrieben. Einzige Auflage: Durch ein fünf Meter breites Tor müssen die Fahrzeuge der Feuerwache, die sich im Hof befindet, auf die Strasse ausfahren können.

Das Preisgericht, dem die Professoren Paul Hofer (Bern), Dolf Schnebli und Ernst Studer (beide ETH Zürich) angehörten, tagte im Oktober/November 1981. Im Dezember waren die Projekte in Basel ausgestellt. Eine Dokumentation mit Darstellungen aller 137 Projekte wird das Baudepartement des Kantons Basel-Stadt im Februar herausgeben.

Und das Ergebnis? Was hat einheimisches Architekturschaffen zur Schliessung einer Altstadt-Baulücke anzubieten? Es ist von keiner architektonischen Entdeckung zu berichten, eher von verwirrender Vielfalt. Das Ergebnis ist im Überblick eine grosse Zitatensammlung, ein Kompendium der Baustile, historischer (von Renaissance bis Jugendstil und Art déco) und moderner (von Gropius über Mies und Wright bis Venturi). Alles scheint möglich.

Einige Beispiele sind auf dieser Doppelseite abgebildet. Ich habe sie unabhängig vom Jury-Entscheid ausgewählt in der Absicht, die wichtigsten Typen von Vorschlägen zu zeigen und damit die Breite des Spektrums anzudeuten. Natürlich habe ich bei jedem Typus jenes Beispiel herausgegriffen, das mich am meisten überzeugt hat.   *Rudolf Schilling*

Lücke bleibt Lücke: Mit einem Gerüst wird die Baulücke noch deutlicher als solche markiert. «Hier ist ein Loch», meldet das Gestänge. Prominenteste Vertreter dieser sogenannten «postmodernen» Architektursprache sind die Amerikaner Venturi & Rauch. (Projekt von Walter Tüscher und Michel Voillat, Architekten BSA, Freiburg.)

Kristallpalästchen: Das Glashaus steht selbstbewusst in der historischen Front. «Ich bin ein Neubau; bin ich nicht elegant?» Der Vorschlag steht in der Tradition der Stahl-Glas-Architektur, deren berühmtester Vertreter Mies van der Rohe ist. (Projekt von Ernst und Beth Stocker, Basel).

Öko-Architektur: Der gläserne Körper hat eine doppelte Haut und ist eventuell mit Sonnenkollektoren ausgerüstet: ein Energiesparhaus. Die äussere Gliederung erinnert an die neogotische Bauweise des deutschen Architekten Gottfried Böhm. (Projekt von Jürg B. Grunder, Architekt HTL Ostermundigen, und Rolf von Allmen, Architekt HTL, Bolligen.)

Neoklassizismus: *Diese breitschultrige Fassadengrafik verwendet klassische Formen: Rundbogen, Quadrat, Säule, Fries. Sie ist ein Beispiel für den aktuellen Trend, monumentale Elemente der Architektur Roms und der Renaissance neu anzuwenden. (Projekt von Felix Schwarz, Rolf Gutmann, Hans Schüpach und Frank Gloor, Architekten BSA/SIA, Basel und Zürich.)*

Dorf in der Stadt: *Als wäre eine Scheune umgebaut worden! Neben die Stadttradition stellt sich die Landtradition. Es soll in der City genau wie im Autobahnrestaurant ein bisschen nach Heu riechen. Seldwyla vertreibt den Überdruss an der Modernität. (Projekt von Trix und Robert Haussmann, Architekten, Zürich; vom Preisgericht angekauft.)*

Überbrückung: *Die angrenzenden Bauten werden über die Lücke verlängert. Beidseits wird «angestrickt». Der neue Teil verfliesst in die alten Teile. Der Vorschlag ist ein Beispiel für das Bemühen um möglichst perfekte Stadtreparatur. (Projekt von Bernhard Hoesli, Jürg Jansen und Stephan Lucek, Architekten ETH/SIA, Zürich.)*

Urbaner Traditionalismus: *Ein nobles Stadthaus stellt sich in die Lücke. Die Architektur nimmt spielerisch Formelemente der Nachbarhäuser auf und verwandelt sie in Spät-Jugendstil. Der Neubau passt sich ein, will aber auch prächtig sein. «Bin ich nicht das schönste Haus in der ganzen Strasse?» (Projekt von René Haubensak, Architekt BSA, Zürich.)*

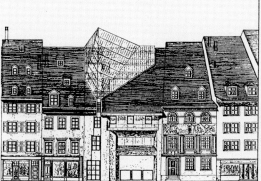

Bio-Architektur: *Die Baulücke wächst zu. Der Eindruck entsteht, von beiden Seiten habe es kräftig und mächtig zu wuchern begonnen. Ein bisschen spielt diese Organik auf Frank Lloyd Wright oder eventuell auf Rudolf Steiner an. (Projekt von Florian Vischer und Georges Weber, Architekten BSA, Basel.)*

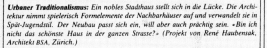
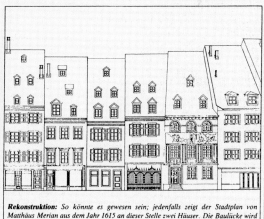

Rekonstruktion: *So könnte es gewesen sein; jedenfalls zeigt der Stadtplan von Matthäus Merian aus dem Jahr 1615 an dieser Stelle zwei Häuser. Die Baulücke wird historisch so geschlossen, wie es denkmalpflegerisch plausibel scheint. Ergebnis: Es gab sie gar nie, diese Baulücke. (Projekt von Heinz Forster, Architekt HTL/STV, Frauenfeld.)*

The building gap as playing field for the game of the city; article from the *Zürcher Tages Anzeiger*'s magazine insert, January 16, 1982.

Translation see p. 203–204 [8]

AN AIRPORT: KLOTEN NEAR ZURICH

Kloten Airport, Switzerland's largest airport on the outskirts of Zurich, is yet another palimpsest, a text that has been overwritten repeatedly, sequenced and layered like the acts of a play. The current structure's gestalt clearly reflects the ever-changing needs, goals, and dreams of the city's inhabitants. In the beginning, the airport was a window onto the great wide world. Then in a second phase, it became a monument to modern functionality. In a third phase, the window onto the world was nailed shut and the airport became a commonplace transportation center. Finally, in its most recent incarnation, Kloten has become a temple of aesthetics. In its fifty-year history, the airport eagerly absorbed each new phase of emerging energy, becoming in the process a continually altered piece of the city.

Kloten Airport opened in April 1953. An editorial in the local daily paper, the *Neue Zürcher Zeitung*, noted at the time: "The rendezvous of nations will unfold in spectacular fashion in the splendid setting of the new airport and transform Kloten into a locale that is unequalled far and wide ... Upon entering the terminal, one is positively prepared for the imminent event of air travel." 9

As part of its latest transformation, a new terminal called Dock Midfield opened at Kloten Airport. Swiss architect Marc Angélil, who planned the Midfield terminal in collaboration with Martin Spühler, writes about the project:

"The ... aforementioned trends in airport design – that is, the monotony of banal efficiency as well as the intrusive celebration of form – are not only expressions of similar cultural and economic principles, but also exert a nearly identical anesthetic effect on the viewer. The term anesthetic, which Wolfgang Welsch understands as the reverse of aesthetics, refers to the condition that nullifies the 'perceptive faculty.' Instead of

Kloten Airport, Zurich, 1950

promoting sensory perception, anesthetics contribute to creating 'a lack of feeling' in the viewer – 'in the sense of a loss,' as Welsch puts it, 'a suppression or the impossibility of sensibility.' This situation presents an opportunity for architecture to oppose the anaesthetization, to withstand it by promoting a critical relationship with reality based in perception. This task, which demands a developed aesthetic thinking and action, requires an extraordinarily deep understanding of the system of forces, which ... determines the production of space in all its aspects, including those factors that have an anaesthetizing effect." [10]

These architects' perspective produced a building that is radically removed from the banal efficiency of the third building phase, the technical functionality of the second phase and linear ideology of progress that characterized the airport in its first phase. It has the characteristics of a building that belongs in the beyond-the-modern era: multiplicity, poetry, sensuousness and – in the words of one of its creators, Marc Angélil – a "simplicity, in which complex relationships are absorbed and their fundamental characteristics are translated into architecture." [11]

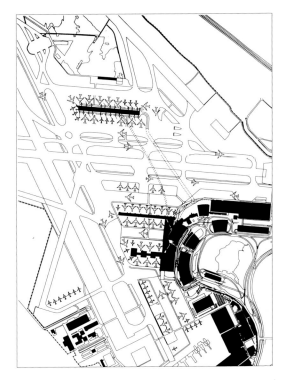

Kloten Airport, Zurich, 2004

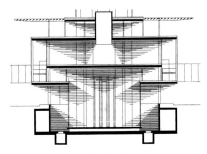

Section of the new Dock Midfield

Dock Midfield, designed by architect Martin Spühler and Zurich's Angélil/Graham/Pfenninger/Scholl Architecture

CARL FINGERHUTH

Kostengerecht und pflegeleicht: Genügt das?

1953: Flughafen Zürich-Kloten, seit 1975 Terminal A. Der Flug-gast erkennt Schweizer Qualität, dezent und sorgfältig.

Was der Präsident des Regierungsrates des Kantons Zürich anlässlich der Eröffnung des Fingerdocks des Flughafens Kloten leider nicht hat sagen können.

An der Eröffnung der Wiener Oper soll sich Kaiser Franz Joseph kritisch über den Neubau geäussert haben. Der beauftragte Architekt nahm sich kurz darauf das Leben. Bei allen Einweihungen von öffentlichen Bauten soll Franz Joseph in der Folge nur noch gesagt haben: «Es war sehr schön. Es hat mich sehr gefreut.»

Bei der Eröffnung des neuen Fingerdocks des Flughafens Kloten im letzten Herbst hat man in den offiziellen Reden lobend festgestellt, dass der Bau termingerecht fertiggestellt wurde und äusserst pflegeleicht sei. Zur architektonischen Gestaltung wurde kein Wort verloren. Bestanden Befürchtungen, der Architekt würde sich sonst ein Leid antun?

Man sagt, jedes Volk habe die Regierung, die es verdiene. Es hat wohl auch die Architektur, die es verdient. In den Bauten jeder Zeit spiegelt sich die entsprechende gesellschaftliche, wirtschaftliche und kulturelle Situation. Das Zürcher

CARL FINGERHUTH, Architekt BSA, führte über viele Jahre ein Architektur- und Planungsbüro in Zürich und ist heute Kantonsbaumeister des Kantons Basel-Stadt.

Volk des frühen Mittelalters hat zur Ehre Gottes das Grossmünster errichtet. Später hat das Zürcher Bürgertum durch den Bau eines repräsentativen Rathauses seinen Machtanspruch dokumentiert. Vor dem Zweiten Weltkrieg gewannen die jungen Architekten Haefeli, Moser und Steiger den Wettbewerb für das Kongresshaus. An prominentester Lage am Seeufer von Zürich wurde mit neuer Architektur Weltoffenheit und Zukunftsgläubigkeit demonstriert. Architektur war immer Geschichtsschreibung.

Auch an den verschiedenen Bauetappen des Flughafens Kloten lässt sich Geschichte ablesen: 1953 wird der Terminal A eingeweiht. Der Bau steht in der Tradition bester Schweizer Architektur der dreissiger bis fünfziger Jahre: Salvisberg, Hofmann, Baur – eine ausserordentlich sorgfältige Gesamtgestaltung vom Konzept bis zum Detail. Vorfahrt, Treppengeländer, Bodenbelag oder der Kontrollturm sind von gleicher Qualität und bilden ein Gesamtwerk. Eine grosszügige helle Halle öffnet sich mit einem hohen Fenster auf die grosse weite Welt. Der Bau bringt in seiner architektonischen Sprache mit weitgehend traditionellen Elementen Optimismus, Zukunftsgläubigkeit, aber in der Pflege des Details auch Sorgfalt

1975: Terminal B. Eine internationale Architekturmaschine. Der Benutzer erkennt sofort: Gleich wie alle andern auch!

1985: Fingerdock. Der Fluggast erkennt am Dutzenddesign eine preiswerte, pflegeleichte, funktionierende Maschine.

1953: Flughafen Zürich-Kloten, die damalige Halle. Gepflegte architektonische Details und ein Blick in die weite Welt.

1975: Terminal B, Abflughalle. Internationales Design, perfekte Organisation, emotionslos und glitzrig wie überall.

1985: Fingerdock, ein termingerecht vollendeter Zu- und Durchgang. Jedes Volk hat die Architektur, die es verdient.

zum Ausdruck. Er zeigt, dass das Zusammenwirken von Gesamtkonzept und Detail die Qualität des Ganzen bestimmt. Der Terminal A wurde eindeutig als ein Schweizer Bauwerk gelesen. Er entstand in einer Tradition von hoher Baukultur und Verpflichtung der Bauherrschaft zu dieser Kultur. Charakteristisch für die Zeit war auch, dass anscheinend an keine Erweiterung gedacht wurde. Es gab im politischen Bewusstsein noch keine exponentiellen Wachstumskurven. Mit dem realisierten Bau glaubte man, das Problem Flughafen für immer gelöst zu haben.

In den späten sechziger Jahren, als man an die Planung der nächsten Etappe ging, hatte sich die Situation wesentlich geändert: keine Grenzen des Wachstums, Wohlstand der öffentlichen Hand, Internationalismus. Der Terminal B wurde zu einer internationalen Architekturmaschine. Keine emotionalen Gesten, keine Ausblicke mehr in die grosse weite Welt, aber gekonntes Design und alles bis zur Perfektion organisiert – nicht zu unterscheiden von anderen internationalen Flughäfen in Afrika oder Amerika.

1975 musste eine weitere Erweiterung der Gesamtanlage geplant werden. Die Gesten von 1953 interessierten nicht mehr, die serielle Gestaltungsqualität von 1975 war zum goldenen Kalb geworden.

1985 wurde das Fingerdock eröffnet. Die Baukosten beliefen sich auf 300 Millionen Franken. Bei Spitzenbelastung entspricht der Energieverbrauch einer Stadt mit 10 000 Einwohnern. Pro Stunde sind 350 000 Ku-

bikmeter Frischluft aufzubereiten. Von aussen sieht man eine schwebende Betonkiste mit einem Kontrollturm, der einer billigen Kaffeemaschine gleicht. Innen herrscht eine Lagerhausstimmung ohne jede Ambiance, ohne jeden Bezug zur Funktion oder zum Ort.

Der Präsident des Regierungsrates hat in seiner Eröffnungsansprache die Chance nicht gehabt, von einem weiteren Beitrag der öffentlichen Hand zur schweizerischen Architekturkultur zu sprechen: «In der Tradition der Bahnhofbauten der Jahrhundertwende, der PTT-Bauten der letzten Jahre im Raum Zürich und Luzern, der Tunnelportale der Nationalstrassen im Tessin hat die Bauherrschaft sich bemüht, ein Werk zu schaffen, das ihrer kulturellen Verpflichtung gerecht wird. Es soll unser Engagement für eine menschliche Gestaltung der Umwelt dokumentieren, eine Gestaltung, die den emotionalen Bedürfnissen der Menschen entspricht. Das Werk soll zeigen, dass Architektur mit kultureller Verantwortung mehr ist als nur Funktion und Solidität. Der Bau soll aber vor allem auch nach aussen wirken. Die Reisenden aus aller Welt sollen sehen, dass wir nicht nur eine termin- und kostengerecht konstruierte und pflegeleicht zu betreibende Welt schaffen wollen.»

Schade, dass dieser Teil der Rede nicht gehalten werden konnte. Als Trost bleibt die Gewissheit, dass beim Abbruch des Fingerdocks der Heimatschutz wahrscheinlich keinen Unterschutzstellungsantrag einreichen wird.

BILDER HANS-PETER SIFFERT PHOTOSWISSAIR COMET

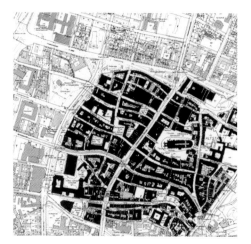

The dense medieval city with its interaction of lanes, deep narrow lots, and public buildings

Urban neighborhoods dominated by streetside development during the capitalistic modernism of the turn of the last century

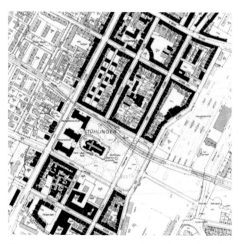

The city of the 1970s: a visionary new city with "optimal supply of light, air, sun, and optimal car access for all buildings"[13]

AN URBAN DISTRICT: RIESELFELD IN FREIBURG, GERMANY

Taking objects out of context, removing them from their element or system, is a particularly modernist tendency. We live in a time of unparalleled interest in individual buildings – never before have we dedicated so much thought, discourse, and publication space to the subject – and yet the subject of cities as a whole is rarely broached. Although certain urban structures may escape the rapid pace of change, most cities are constantly sprouting new sections while old structures become fundamentally transformed. Much like the gestalt of an individual building, or the complex configuration of an airport, the gestalt of a city's urban plan is determined by our current set of values and how those relate to time and place. To help clarify this concept, I will include several town-planning examples. The first deals with Freiburg, a small city in the Breisgau region of southern Germany. The city is one of many founded in southern Germany and Switzerland by the Zähringer dynasty in the early Middle Ages. Today, Freiburg has become a city whose urban structure, over time, has become a virtual guidebook to its history.

The romantic project by Lucien Kroll, Brussels

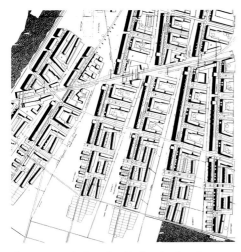

The green project by Tegnestuen Vandkunsten, Copenhagen

The social project by Jochen Dittus, Freiburg; Walter Freter,
Herrischried; Jochen Karl, Schwanau; Reiner Probst, Freiburg

Klaus Humpert was Freiburg's town planner
for eighteen years. He was one of the first
in the beyond-the-modern era to practice
respect for the plot structure of old European
cities. Freiburg was therefore one of the few
cities in post-World War II Germany where
the traditional scale of the city's center was
treated with care. In the 1980s, there was
a steady increase in demand for new housing
within the city that couldn't be met through
further development, or densification. In 1991,
the municipal council agreed to plan a new
urban neighborhood for twelve thousand
inhabitants outside the existing urban
boundaries.

A competition was announced and the
subsequent submissions strongly reflected
the prevailing values of urbanism at that
time. The four proposals shown here each interpreted a major – old or new – theme.
I found it fascinating to observe how the representatives of the different political parties
in the jury identified the proposals that most
closely corresponded to their own dogma
and how they then proceeded to passionately
defend those proposals.

Brussels native Lucien Kroll's romantic project
was eliminated in the second round. Many
were enthused by Kroll's romanticism but
none wanted to take it seriously. It seemed in-
sufficiently robust in the face of the city's
political reality.

The representatives of the Bourgeois
Party put their faith in the traditional city
model proposed by firms Böwer, Eith,
Murken, Spiecker of Freiburg; Güdemann from
Lörrach; and Morlock, Schallstadt, Meier from
Freiburg. Order, clarity, and growth were this
project's leading principles. It demonstrated
easy marketability and included
unhindered vehicle access.

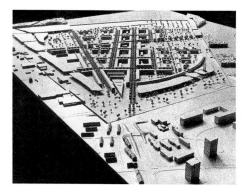

The bourjeois project by Böwer, Eith, Murken, Freiburg; Güdemann, Lörrach; Morlock, Schallstadt, Meier, Freiburg

The Green Party supported the project submitted by the Copenhagen-based firm Tegnestuen Vandkunsten. Its emphasis was on individual housing quality, optimal landscape integration, and public transportation, bicycles, and pedestrian traffic rather than cars.

The Social Democrats were convinced that a new urban neighborhood, separate from the old city, that avoided the rigidity of modern urban design and allowed plenty of open space for communal activities, would best satisfy their needs.

I was unable to convince the majority of the jury to explore the progressive qualities of the Green Party's favored project. I was not allowed to question the old values. The Bourgeois project was chosen instead. Once this decision had been made, the Bourgeois representatives graciously lent their support to the Green project by awarding it second prize. The project's progressive nature was recognized and no one had to act on it. In the end, the Social Democrats had to content themselves with the third prize.
The process, in my opinion, was a missed opportunity.

Mid-construction, 1996

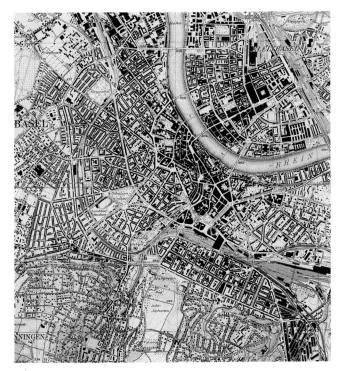

The city of Basel as "frozen history"

A CITY: BASEL

In his work, the German philosopher Jean Gebser tried to provide an "account of ... a new consciousness ... based on insights into mankind's mutations from its primordial beginnings up to the present." [14] It continues to surprises me how frequently philosophical writings relate to our interplay with cities. In his seminal work *The Ever-Present Origin*, Gebser wrote: "Before we can discern the new, we must know the old. The adage that everything has already happened, that there is nothing new under the sun (and the moon), is only conditionally correct. It is true that everything has always been there, but in another way, in another light, with a different value attached to it, in another realization or manifestation." [15]

I stated earlier that cities evolve out of the constant interaction between society and space:

– In the first example, Basel's Spalenvorstadt, this involved the insertion of a new building into an existing urban structure.
– In the second example, Zürich Airport, this took place through the step-by-step extension and transformation of an existing structure.
– In the third example, Freiburg's Rieselfeld, it occurred through the new development of a space that had not yet been claimed by the city.
– Finally, evolution may also take the form of city-wide transformation.

This transformation always occurs, as Gebser wrote, "in another way, in another light, with a different value attached to it, in another realization or manifestation." When evolution occurs, eras become crystallized and lie side by side like ice floes, or one on top of the other, like geological layers. The development of the Spalenvorstadt building gap took four years, the construction of the new neighborhood in Freiburg's Rieselfeld took over ten years. The four layers of Kloten Airport evolved over a fifty-year period. In the case of the city of Basel, the timeframe was two thousand years. Thus, I view Basel as a large geological museum. Antiquity, early and late Middle Ages, the modern age, and the present are deposited in the permafrost of the city. To clarify, I must briefly document what Goethe described as Basel's "frozen history."

The celtic layer

Varying rock densities, tectonic shifts, and the Rhine river's natural watercourse created favorable conditions for a human settlement. The city of Basel was first created at a spot where the Rhine could be crossed in relative safety and the surrounding hills could be fortified by simple means. Shortly before the beginning of the Christian or Common Era, a first urban settlement was therefore created on the south bank of the Rhine. The Celtic tribe later retreated to a hill on the bank of the Rhine and created a fortified space to protect its inhabitants. This primary layer defines the structure of Basel's innercity to this day.

The early medieval layer

In the early Middle Ages, the Münster hill was expanded by a second, organic network of roads aligned with the central church. The lanes and squares evolved in response to the topography, the hill, and the river. Around 1200 AD, the town had become too cramped and a new city – today still known as Kleinbasel, or Lesser Basel – was erected on the north bank of the Rhine. It displays the same rigorously organized, right-angled town structure as the old German city of Freiburg in the Breisgau.

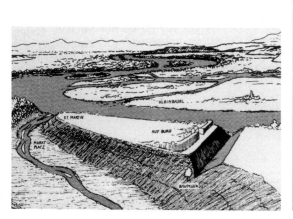

The late medieval layer

The third major change occurred around 1400. Once again there was too little space in the city. Without altering the existing street grid and lot structure, a new and larger fortification belt was built around the city. The gates were moved farther out along the main roads leading out of the city. So-called suburbs grew between the old and new gates. The size of this newly demarcated territory combined with low population growth rates, political stability, and few technological innovations between 1400 and 1800, resulted in a city structure that remained virtually unchanged for four hundred years.

The nineteenth-century layer

In the mid-nineteenth century, industrialization and new transportation technology drew thousands of people into the city. Having developed on the basis of the old social, economic, and cultural system, the city was unable to integrate this sudden growth. A new gestalt had to be found to accommodate the new era. The greatest resistance came from the unsuitable plot allotment of the old system of land ownership. To allow for rapid expansion, this system had to be transformed. The pattern remained the same: a system of streets, lots, and public and private land governed by specific rules. However, new legal tools had to be invented to implement the new dynamic of the time. The building line and expropriation made this possible. For the first time in centuries, a new city could evolve without consideration for property ownership and historic paths. A new city plan was drafted, authorized, and built.

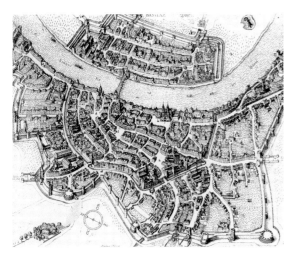

The twentieth-century layer

The fifth transformation was again the result of a technical and economic revolution. The invention of the gasoline engine replaced public transportation and required that the city's density be somewhat relieved and its roadways widened. The rapid growth of the gross national product generated universal wealth, which allowed many people from different socio-economic backgrounds to purchase cars and single-family homes. The nineteenth-century city rapidly spilled out across the landscape, with new street and building-lot structures, and with, in Gebser's words, "a different value attached to it, in another realization or manifestation."

The next layer

The city's current regional development plan displays the first efforts to deal with the complexity and contradiction of the existing city in a creative and conscious way. The city's many overlapping historical layers are considered an opportunity for transformation. The new is no longer simply built next to the old. The goal is not to demolish and build new urban quarters but to reinterpret them, as is being done with the St. Albanquartier, Luzernerring, the master plan for the SBB Railway Station, the Gundeldinger neighborhood, the Basel Fair, and the German Railway's freight station. But a new relationship between the city and its surrounding landscape is also emerging, although it remains difficult to discern within the densely developed city limits.

Herzog & de Meuron's design for the expansion of Basel's
St. Jakob stadium

Project for the development of the Miba site on St. Jakobstrasse.
The competition was won by Basel-based firm Diener & Diener.

Urban concept for assigning a new use to Basel's Deutsche
Bahn freight depot. The firm Ernst Niklaus Fausch from
Aarau, Switzerland won the competition.

Transformation of the Gundeldinger neighborhood: short-listed
proposal for development of the area at the end of the new station
overpass by architects Cruz-Ortiz/Giraudi-Wettstein, Seville and
Lugano. Basel's Herzog & de Meuron won the competition.

INTEGRAL CONSCIOUSNESS

We cannot discuss urbanism in the beyond-the-modern era without exploring the uniqueness of the age we live in today. To do so, I shall follow in the footsteps of Jean Gebser and Ken Wilber. In *The Ever-Present Origin*, Jean Gebser introduces us to five principle levels of consciousness and discusses how they evolved. Each of these epochs generates a unique worldview developed on the basis of common needs, goals, and dreams – in other words, out of the thought, sensibility, sensitivity, and intuition of the respective epoch. "Every mutation of consciousness that constituted a new structure of consciousness was accompanied by the appearance and effectuality of a new dimension." [16]

The oldest level of consciousness is defined as archaic. This level is followed by the magical, the mythical, and finally the mental, or modern era. According to Gebser, the current era is showing the first signs of something radically new, a period he refers to as integral. This era is just beginning to emerge. Its aspects are still only partially formulated and, in our still very rational times, remain difficult to pinpoint. At the same time, many view the prospect of a new era, with all its strange and unknown phenomena, as a serious existential threat to our cities and culture.

Whereas archaic, magical, mythical, and modern have become familiar terms for describing an era, employing the term integral as a blanket term for the coming era presents difficulties. The term postmodern was introduced in European theoretical writings at the beginning of the twentieth century. It was soon also adopted in philosophy and other areas of science and culture. Most modern Westerners, however, first experienced postmodernism as it related to the gestalt of cities. In the 1970s, architects became annoyed with the concept of postmodernism and, rather than viewing it as the herald of a new era, they interpreted it as a direct affront to great modernist truths. Without much reflection about its potential, postmodernism was fundamentally discredited in the context of dealing with the city. Thus, to avoid the negative implications of the term postmodernism, I have decided to describe the period we live in today as the beyond-the-modern age. In the following paragraphs, I will attempt to outline how we reached this stage.

STRUCTURE SPACE AND TIME RELATIONSHIP

	Dimensioning	Perspectivity	Emphasis
Archaic:	Zero-dimensional	None	Prespatial / Pretemporal
Magical:	One-dimensional	Pre-perspectival	Spaceless / Timeless
Mythical:	Two-dimensional	Unperspectival	Spaceless / Natural temporal
Mental:	Three-dimensional	Perspectival	Spatial / Abstractly temporal
Integral:	Four-dimensional	Aperspectival	Space-free / Time-free

From *The Ever-Present Origin*, by Jean Gebser

The archaic period

In the archaic period, man had not yet developed a consciousness of self. He lived in a paradise where every emerging form – human, animal, and vegetable – was continuously absorbed into the great cycle of life. Neither space nor time was consciously perceived. A few bones, stone axes, and some fossilized footprints in what was then soft soil, are the only physical traces that remain of this time. The memory of this period survives in our existing imagery of paradise and in our tales about noble savages.

The prehistoric Neanderthal footprint in the loam of a cave near Toirano, Italy

Adam and Eve in the Garden of Eden in Hieronymus Bosch's
The Garden of Earthly Delights, 1477

The Earth goddess

The magical period

While their consciousness was still rooted in the forces of nature, the people of the magical period had lost their innocence. Their perception of the world can still be seen today in their cave wall drawings. Here, amidst their sagas and rituals, we see the first signs of interaction with the foreign, the unknown, the devil, death, space, and time. The first boundaries are drawn between the self and the menacing other.

A consciousness of place evolves: in the desert...

...on water...

...and in a rock face. [17]

The magician in the cave of Trois Frères: man and nature are "not yet differentiated but still magically merged."

The mythical period

The transition into the mythical period was accompanied by an enormous expansion of human consciousness. The individual soul had been discovered and was integrated into a religion that connected body, soul, and spirit. Spirits became deities, hordes and clans became dynasties, and chiefs became kings.

At the same time, villages and settlements became cities and spatial differentiations began to emerge between the public and the private, sacred and commonplace, rich and poor. Mankind began anchoring itself to specific space, thereby linking heaven and earth. Cities were established. In the process, urban spaces were given structural order and symbolic form, largely determined by the exploration of time and its rootedness in space.

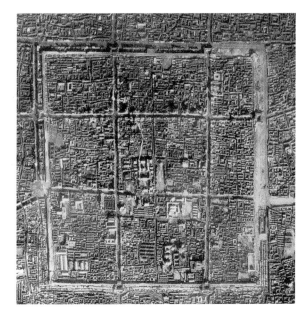

Cities begin to develop around the globe: in Mukden, China...

...in Priene, Greece...

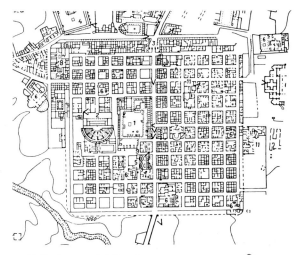

...and in the Roman empire's Timgad.

The mental period

In modernism, the mental period is considered the greatest step in the evolution of human consciousness. With time, however, self-awareness became increasingly reduced to rational consciousness. Thus modern cities were based on discoveries and awareness distinctly influenced by the constructs of the mental period: technology, the exclusion of nature, control, order, rationality, functionality, and economics.

This type of city was described as early as 1637 by philosopher René Descartes: "There is often not so much perfection in works composed of many pieces and made by the hands of various master craftsmen as there is in those works on which but a single individual has worked. Thus one sees that buildings undertaken and completed by a single architect are usually more attractive and better ordered than those that many architects have tried to patch up by using old walls that had been built for other purposes. Thus those ancient cities that were once mere villages and in the course of time have become large towns are usually so poorly laid out, compared to those well-ordered places that an engineer traces out on a vacant plain as it suits his fancy, that even though, upon considering each building one by one in the former sort, one often finds as much, if not more, art than one finds in those of the latter sort, Still, upon seeing how the buildings are arranged – here a large one, there a small one – and how they make the streets crooked and uneven, one would say that it is chance rather than the will of some men using reason that has arranged them thus." [18]

Como, Berne, Philadelphia, Washington, Karlsruhe, Manhattan, Berlin, Brasilia, and Halle-Neustadt are characterized by this approach.

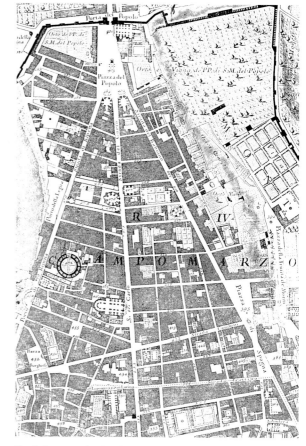

The city becomes ordered: Nolli plan of Rome, 1748...

...and controlled: Ernst May, Westhausen development in Frankfurt on Main, 1929-1931

The integral period, or the beyond-the-modern era

Jean Gebser refers to the beyond-the-modern era as the integral period. He uses such terms as four-dimensional, transparent, aperspectival, acausal, and arational to describe the new era. Physicists Albert Einstein, Werner Heisenberg, and Wolfgang Pauli brought attention to this new era early on. With the 1975 publication of *The Tao of Physics*, Fritjof Capra captured mainstream attention by exploring the parallels between modern physics and Eastern philosophies. In my view, Ken Wilber and Rupert Sheldrake formulated the most comprehensive accounts on the subject in recent years. Science has begun, Sheldrake writes, "to transcend the mechanistic world-view. The idea that everything is determined in advance and in principle predictable has given way to the ideas of indeterminism, spontaneity and chaos. The invisible organizing powers of nature are once again emerging in the form of fields. The hard, inert atoms of Newtonian physics have dissolved into structures of vibratory activity. The uncreative world machine has turned into a creative, evolutionary cosmos. Even the *laws* of nature may not be eternally fixed; they may be evolving along with nature."[19]

A new worldview is indeed emerging, accompanied by its own lexicon of terms. Sheldrake continues: "At each level, holons are wholes containing parts, which are themselves wholes containing lower-level parts, and so on. The diagram could, for example, represent subatomic particles in atoms, in molecules, in crystals; or cells in tissues, in organs, in organisms; or planets in solar systems, in galaxies, in galactic clusters; or phonemes in words, in phrases, in sentences."[20] Or, one might add, in the rooms, houses, blocks, urban neighborhoods, cities, and metropolises which, together, form the holarchic systems that create the great game of the city.

The city begins to grow beyond the scope of control...

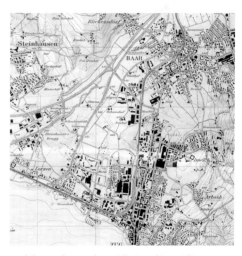

...and the complexity and contradictions of its gestalt informs its constant transformation.

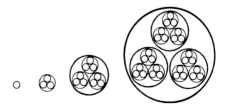

With the tiered hierarchy of its morphological units, it can be interpreted as a holon.

Villa of a former Red Army general in Hong Kong.
My niece, Lisina Fingerhuth, planned the project after
studying with Hans Kollhof in Berlin.

—

THE GREATEST PRODUCTS OF ARCHITECTURE ARE LESS THE WORKS OF INDIVIDUALS THAN OF SOCIETY; ... THE RESIDUE OF SUCCESSIVE EVAPORATIONS OF HUMAN SOCIETY.

— *Victor Hugo* [21]

02

THE MODERN CITY

So far, I have attempted to demonstrate how throughout time, a city's gestalt reflects its inhabitants' existential aspirations. Now I wish to explore how the birth and evolution of a new era, defined by a new consciousness, requires a thoroughly fresh understanding of our cities. Finally, I will explore the transformation of cities in the beyond-the-modern era based on the major principles of Taoist philosophy.

The modern era is one of the great periods in the evolution of human consciousness. It highlighted our journey from a mythical world into a mental one. Two major themes influenced this transformation. One theme was our fascination with the rational. Prior to the modern era, evolution was about exploring the depth and breadth of our human potential. The scope of human perception became broadened. Modernism, by contrast, concerned itself primarily with the mental dimension. This required a drastic narrowing down, or focusing, of our human energies of perception. Humankind had to restrict other aspects of its being – sensibility, emotion, spirituality – in favor of rationality. The other theme was the liberation of humankind from the bonds of collectivity. The demagogic culture of the late Middle Ages had to be overthrown. Inspired by heroic figures of the Renaissance – Galileo, Michelangelo, and Erasmus of Rotterdam – science, art, and philosophy became valued as autonomous disciplines. This differentiation liberated us. It led to the creation of democratic Western societies, the struggle against racial and gender-based discrimination, and the establishment of human rights. It gave the sciences autonomy from the church and enabled individuals to follow their own spiritual paths. Art was liberated from the collective rule of sovereigns so that artists became free to explore their emotions and spirituality. Both themes, however, would eventually become exhausted. In the late modern period, science, and hence technology, took center stage. Art and philosophy were discriminated against and reduced to elective disciplines. But when mental nature is allowed to rule supreme, it has the power to destroy. The same applies to human individuality: The reintegration of human spirituality means that we must reintegrate the individual human being, on a higher level, into a new general consciousness.

In the beyond-the-modern era, we have the opportunity to expand our horizon, not at the expense of what we know, but as a renaissance, a rebirth that integrates all the formerly excluded aspects of our consciousness on a new and broader platform.

THE DIGNITY OF MODERNISM AND ITS CITIES

Architects' perception of modernism is less founded in its development over time than in its formal expression. Criticism of the most negative aspects of modernism is therefore largely dismissed. This becomes evident upon exploring the beginnings of architectural modernism. Perhaps the last discipline among Western sciences, art, and philosophy to do so, architecture only discovered modernism after World War I.

From a philosophical perspective, the European modern period originated in Athens with the philosophy of Socrates, Plato, and Aristotle. Plato's teaching about the importance of ideas becomes the basis for a new era. It is founded in the assumption that sensual perception can only produce illusory opinion. Thus only terms that reference ideas can provide security.

Plato's cave

The School of Athens, glorified by Raphael in 1509, with Plato standing center-left and Aristotle center-right

From an art history perspective, the modern era was launched with the work of Florentine painter and architect Giotto di Bondone and substantially reinforced by Michelangelo. Giotto's work marked the beginning of a different way of representing the world, a personal viewpoint, a central perspective that lent form and meaning. Michelangelo then took the next step. He depicts the individual human position and makes man God's partner on earth. People begin to see themselves as autonomous beings.

From a scientific perspective, the modern era begins with Copernicus and Galileo. Their discovery that the earth is in fact a planet within the solar system liberated humankind from the confines of terrestrial space. Space suddenly became infinitely vast and people had to come to terms with the fact that its borders are intangible.

Galileo presents his telescope to the Doge of Venice.

The Expulsion of the Demons from Arezzo, 1299, painted by Giotto in a perspective drawing of the city

The Creation of Man as God's partner, painted by Michelangelo around 1512 on the ceiling of the Sistine Chapel

Illustration from Descartes' *Discourse on Method and Meditations on First Philosophy*

From yet another philosophical perspective, the modern age began in the first half of the seventeenth century when René Descartes formulated his scientific worldview. He envisioned the world as a mechanical apparatus which, once switched on, would continue functioning automatically.

From a technological perspective, Scotsman James Watt's development of the steam engine marked the beginning of the modern era. It made modernism's technology-driven economic revolution possible. There appeared to be unlimited potential for growth.

Rain, Steam and Speed – The Great Western Railway, by William Turner, 1843

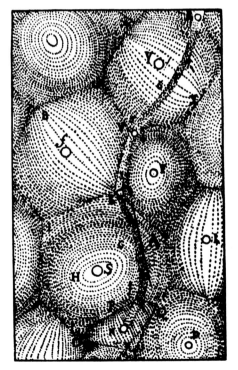

The world as a hydro-dynamic continuum

Steel production at Krupp in Essen, Germany, 1862

From a political perspective, the modern age is rooted in the American and French revolutions. Along with *egalité, fraternité,* and *liberté* for the individual, these uprisings led to the abolition of slavery, defined human rights, and institutionalized the division of political powers.

From an urbanism perspective, mid-nine-teenth-century Paris marked the beginning of the modern age. The deliberately political act of destroying the old city in favor of build-ing large new boulevards set a social process in motion in which Europe broke off from the gestalt of the medieval city. A similar process had already prompted the construction with-in the United States of new modern cities such as Washington, Philadelphia, and New York. However, since these cities had been con-structed on open land, without substantial resistance from pre-existing historical city sites, they were barely noted in Europe.

The Declaration of Independence, John Trumbull, 1776

Plan for the city of Washington, 1792

Storming of the Bastille by the people of Paris on July 14, 1789. "The Bastille was a building [that was] emphasized and extremely imperious in character, which symbolized defiance, pride, compulsion, power, invincibility and toughness in a threatening manner."[22]

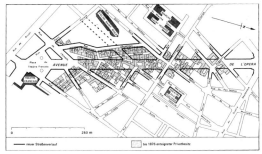
Plan for the construction of the Avenue de l'Opéra in Paris, 1850

From an architectural perspective, the modern age belatedly emerges in the 1920s. Its voice is heard in the French architectural journal *L'Esprit Nouveau*. In the first issue, dated October 1920, Swiss architect and city planner Le Corbusier writes: "Architecture does not manifest itself as the style of an era. Louis XV, XVI, XIV or the Gothic style are to architecture what a feather is on a woman's hat: it may be pretty every now and then, but not always and no more than that." [23] The house is now a machine and the traditional town with its *rue corridor* should be transformed into simple *espace libre*. And so, in a post-World War I era characterized by intense social and political upheaval, modern building discovered its *esprit nouveau* – a gestalt that reflected the desperate struggle for individual freedom and social justice. Architects were the last to integrate modernist principles into their work. This may also be why they remain among the few who, to this day, celebrate it with such determination.

The flagship of modern architecture: Unité d'Habitation by Le Corbusier in Marseilles, France

Residential building by Hans Schmidt in Riehen near Basel, 1929

Building modern cities was a gargantuan task. Architects and city planners had faced a similar challenge in the early Middle Ages. A new way of thinking was required and their response to the challenge endured well into the mid-nineteenth century. Thus, this period too could feature in a discussion about the early Middle-Age beginnings of modernism in urban design and architecture. But the modern city of the twentieth century, while incorporating key elements of the twelfth century city, also had to cope with a multitude of entirely new challenges.

It is one of nineteenth-century society's greatest achievements that it succeeded in developing a new and efficient technical gestalt for its modern cities. Explosive growth within urban areas had created urgent needs for new roads, water supply systems, sewers, and public transportation.

London in 1872 as depicted in an engraving by Gustave Doré

London's Underground in an illustration published by London newspaper *Universal Illustrated*, 1867

Berlin-Charlottenburg, 1909

Another one of modern society's great achievements is the creation of a socially-conscious city. A primary goal was to create housing that respected human dignity. This meant incorporating new urban design principles into the transformation of early modern towns dominated by industrial development. Cities needed social infrastructure. Plenty of town halls, gas factories, railway stations, abattoirs, and barracks had been built in the nineteenth century; now kindergartens, schools, hospitals, hostels, and sports facilities were needed. Finally, the new approach to urban planning required that people be protected from excessive exposure to noise and pollution.

Radburn, New Jersey, built in 1928 by architects Clarence Stein and Henry Wright

Heiligfeld housing development in Zurich, 1950–56, designed by Heinrich Steiner

Satellite cities were seen as a remedy for the problems of large cities that had grown too quickly.

The mass production of automobiles at the beginning of the twentieth century forced even greater urban innovation to accommodate the demands of a new mobility. What first seemed like a minor and rather harmless expansion soon became one of the modern city's greatest challenges. Technological and social modernity would soon become a central focus for modern urban dwellers and cause a radical questioning of the gestalt of early modern cities.

The combination of technological progress, social revolution, and newfound mobility unleashed powerful energies in civic society. But it also initiated a whole series of fascinating cultural processes that, to this day, have yet to be adequately incorporated into the gestalt of our cities.

Parking lot at the Ford factory in Dearborn, Michigan, 1936

Large housing development in Berlin-Marzahn

Buckminster Fuller's US Pavillion at EXPO '67 in Montréal

THE CATASTROPHE OF MODERNISM AND ITS CITIES

Science, rooted in rationality, banishes spiritual knowledge from its realm, discriminates against emotion, and diminishes art to a merely decorative pursuit. When I write of the catastrophe of the modern period, I am by no means ignoring its dignity. I wish simply to present a critical portrayal of the problems of our time. I choose the word catastrophe because I perceive within cities a drastic increase in challenges that can no longer be resolved within modernism's social, economic, and cultural framework. Modernism's differentiation between science, art, and philosophy, led to an increasingly aggressive dissociation from aesthetic, creative, religious, and ethical pursuits. Powerful and monolithic, science colonized and dominated these fields. [24]

The great principles of modernism – truth, the division of subject and object, morality, the separation between nature and man, and the reliability of science – lost their positive momentum and became increasingly negative forces. Virtues that were no longer anchored in the wholeness of humankind became sins. In this sense, thrift became avarice; bravery became aggression; ethical principles became political imperialism. The modern age allowed itself to be monopolized by the mind, resulting in "dissociation, alienation, separation and flattening." [25] Religion and art were increasingly rejected as equal partners and relegated to heaven or hell. Dominant social values required deep anchoring in one-dimensional scientific thought.

In his book *The Ecology of the Mind*, Gregory Bateson described the tragic effects of the modern age thus: "The ideas which dominate our civilization at the present time ... may be summarized as follows:

a) It is us against the environment.
b) It is us against other men.
c) It is the individual (or the individual society or the individual nation) that matters.
d) We can have unilateral control over the environment and must strive for it.
e) We live within infinitely expanding boundaries.
f) Economic determinism is common sense.
g) Technology will do it for us." [26]

The zeitgeist of modern cities was characterized by rigid dogmatism, radical disrespect for existing structures, unquestioned preference for new structures, and a pronounced aggression vis-à-vis irrational ideas. Its paradigm was embedded in an unchallenged quest for perfection and the pursuit of conflict-free purity. As the gestalt of modern cities matured, however, it began to show increasing problems. The new, pure, and gloriously modern city, replete with promises of enhanced health and well-being, began mutating into an asocial, monotonous, commonplace, and violent repository of soulessness.

THE DIFFICULT SIDE OF ORDER

The inherent complexity and contradictions of the world and its cities proved too great a challenge for modern man. In an attempt to escape the chaos of reality, humankind launched a frantic quest for order, transparency, and clarity. Le Corbusier, preeminent apostle of modernism wrote: "Man strides forward in a straight line because he has a goal; he knows where he is going and has chosen a direction. The donkey walks in a zigzag line, takes a little nap, dumb from the heat and, distracted, walks in a zigzag to step around rocks, to make the ascent easier and to seek shade. He makes as little effort as possible." [27]

The scientific mind, disconnected from its emotional and sensory perception and lacking confidence in its intuition, was no longer anchored in the fullness of its being. Emotions became suspect – they lacked objectivity and constancy.
Spirituality, too, could not be trusted because it could not be scientifically tested and proven accurate. Faith became a lost cause. Humankind became deeply alienated from sensuality and emotion. When asked by a peasant woman, during an open house in 1928, why Le Corbusier's building in the Weissenhof housing development in Stuttgart conjoined the lavatory with the living room, architect Alfred Roth reportedly responded: "[because] modern man does not stink!" Roth would later become a renowned professor of architecture at the Swiss Federal Institute of Technology in Zurich.

The pure modern city: Dammerstock, Karlsruhe, Germany, 1928

The pure modern house: Le Corbusier's contribution to Germany's Werkbund exhibition, Weissenhof, Stuttgart, 1927

THE DIFFICULT SIDE OF OBJECTIVITY

Swiss architects Benedikt Huber and Christian Süsstrunk described the importance of objective form to the modern architect thus:
"1. Form must be independent of its architect and time of origin.
2. Form must be calculable and comprehensible.
3. The meaning of form must only refer to its genesis.
4. The evolutionary process of architectural form is complete within itself and defines the only correct and possible form.
Over time, the absoluteness of these maxims could only lead to internal conflicts among its adherents and within the evolution of the architecture. Any further development had to either end in heresy or in a desperate attempt to defend the pure theory of form. The theory of pure form of the *Neues Bauen*, of the modern, was not only put into question by the regression of fascist architecture, the inflation of the economic boom, and the emotional wave of the vernacular style (*Heimatstil*). It was also the absoluteness of the definition itself that could not stand up to the plurality of evolution." [28]

Campaign poster from Basel's "progressive organizations" party, 1978

The deliberate dynamiting of St. Louis' Pruitt-Igoe public housing complex on July 15, 1972 at 3:32 p.m., epitomized this internal conflict. Architect and author Charles Jencks defined this moment as the starting point of post-modernism. In an odd twist of fate, Pruitt-Igoe architect Minoru Yamasaki would later design another building destined for destruction – New York City's World Trade Center. In 1951, the American Institute of Architects recognized the Pruitt-Igoe project with an Outstanding Building Award. The very qualities that were praised – the pedestrian zone and communal areas separated from the ground floor, the rational and pure design (intended to inspire similar virtues in its inhabitants), and the deliberate omission of semi-public spaces – caused the complex to be repeatedly abused by residents to such a degree that there was nothing left to do but demolish it a mere twenty years later.

Blasting the Pruitt-Igoe development (built between 1952–1955), Saint Louis, 1972

THE DIFFICULT SIDE OF PURE THEORY

French architect and urban planner Marcel Lods' sketches are, in my view, the most radical illustrations of the dogma of modern urban design.[29] They vividly celebrate the unequivocal worldview of the modern age and illustrate its main tenets: Order is better than complexity. Light is better than dark. New is better than old. Distance is better than proximity. Clarity is better than lack of clarity. The collective and universal are superior to the individual and particular. Linear processes create better results than cyclical processes.

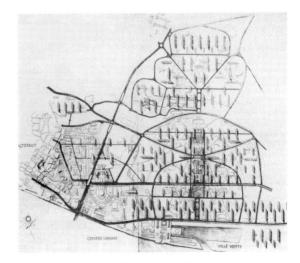

Plan for the reconstruction of the German city of Mainz, by Marcel Lods, 1947

Marcel Lods' sketches illustrating his plan

THE DIFFICULT SIDE OF INNOVATION

"The search for innovation was at once the driving force and the tragic comeuppance of modernism's 'grand narrative'," [30] writes Swiss architecture critic André Bideau. The dedicated search for new structure and form deteriorated into disrespect and destructive aggression toward existing urban structures. This aggression was most fierce when applied to meeting the long-term requirements of automobile transportation.

Images for the new city: in the United States 1924, rendering of Chicago by Ludwig Hilberseimer...

...in France 1925, *Plan Voisin* for the center of Paris by Le Corbusier...

...in England, 1967, as illustrated in *Cars for Cities*. (Here people did more than just talk about the new city. After World War II, they actually built them.) ...

...and in Switzerland, 1933, Carl Moser's plan for Zurich...

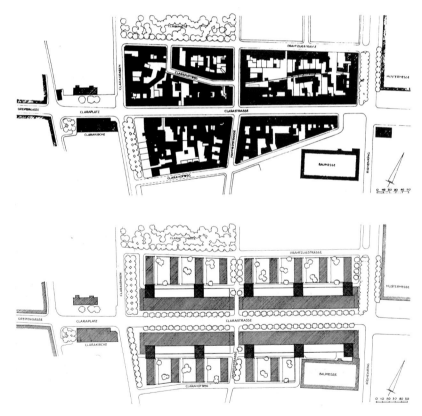

...1946, Hans Schmidt's plan for the demolition of Lesser
Basel's old town

THE FLIP SIDE OF GREAT TRUTH

I find it fascinating that in the 1980s, the purist desire for a specific urban gestalt led to a radically different but equally modernist contention that any kind of intervention into the constructs of cities would prove irreparably destructive. The salvation of the city would no longer be found in perfection but in completeness.

Carl Jung described the paradox of this polarity in *Answer to Job*. "For, just as completeness is always imperfect, so perfection is always incomplete, and therefore represents a final state which is hopelessly sterile ... Perfectionism always ends in a blind alley, while completeness by itself lacks selective values." [32]

The unadulterated, fully-built city thus became mythologized, replacing the prior goal of building utopian, perfect cities. This era was characterized by messianic self-confidence, a radical disrespect for anything new, a desire to fight against any type of new structure, and a pronounced aggression toward rationality. Conversely, this ideology also involved a profound adherence to established values, a dedication to tried and true methods, and a robust belief in the importance of the past. Familiar form and tradition were celebrated for their purity and lack of conflict. This would become known as the antimodern movement.

In 1989, the Prince of Wales wrote: "Is this new development at Richmond by Quinlan Terry merely pastiche? It may look familiar and have an 18th century feeling to it, but it is not just a series of copies of buildings from the past. The architect has used a familiar language to create an expression of harmony and proportion." [31]

A 1970's social housing development in Marne La Vallée, France

Multifamily house on the Löwengasse in Vienna, 1970, designed by Austrian artist Friedensreich Hundertwasser in collaboration with the city of Vienna

Las Vegas

PERHAPS A FITTING REQUIEM FOR THE IRRELEVANT WORKS
OF ART THAT ARE TODAY'S DESCENDENTS OF A ONCE MEANINGFUL
MODERN ARCHITECTURE ARE ELIOT'S LINES IN 'EAST COOKER':
'THAT WAS A WAY OF PUTTING IT – NOT VERY SATISFACTORY:
A PERIPHRASTIC STUDY IN A WORN-OUT POETICAL FASHION,
LEAVING ONE STILL WITH INTOLERABLE WRESTLE
WITH WORDS AND MEANINGS. THE POETRY DOES NOT MATTER.'

— *Venturi | Scott Brown | Izenour* [33]

- Reintegrating consciousness of man's unity with nature;
- Reintegrating the essence of aesthetics.

Here, my premise is in agreement with Küng's reflections. It is all the more important, therefore, to achieve – as Küng writes elsewhere – "a new, liberating, enriching effect" for the city.

The following text by Carl Jung, from the 1929 foreword to his book *The Secret of the Golden Flower*, vividly captures many of the themes that, in our time, can no longer be ignored. Jung also provides a link to China, a country whose ways I also wish to explore here.

03 THE BEYOND-THE-MODERN CITY

THE DIGNITY OF THE BEYOND-THE-MODERN ERA

The purpose of this book is to explore the new dignity currently unfolding in the beyond-the-modern era, a premise supported by many experts outside the field of urbanism. Swiss theologian Hans Küng defined the current movement as "a social shift not against, averse to, science, technology, industry and democracy, but a shift with, in alliance with, these social powers which formerly were absolutized but now have been relativized. The specific values of the industrial modernity – diligence (*industria!*), rationality, order, thoroughness, punctuality, sobriety, achievement, efficiency – are not just to be done away with but to be reinterpreted in a new constellation and combined with the new values of postmodernity: with imagination, sensitivity, emotion, warmth, tenderness, humanity. So it is not a matter of repudiations and condemnations, but of counterbalances, counter-plans, counter-directions and counter-movements." [34]

In the foreword to this book, I outlined the major themes of the beyond-the-modern era and city. These include:
- Reintegrating the non-rational dimension of human existence;
- Reintegrating consciousness of the polarity of all existence;

"For a long time, spirit, and the passion of the spirit, were the greatest values and the things most worth striving for in our peculiar Christian culture of the mind. Only after the decline of the Middle Ages, that is, in the course of the nineteenth century, when spirit began to degenerate into intellect, there set in a reaction against the unbearable domination of intellectualism which led to the pardonable mistake of confusing intellect with spirit, and blaming the latter for the misdeeds of the former. Intellect does, in fact, violate the soul when it tries to possess itself of the heritage of the spirit. It is in no way fitted to do this, because spirit is something higher than intellect in that it includes not only the latter, but the feelings as well. It is a line or principle of life that strives after superhuman, shining heights; but, in opposition to it, stands the dark, earth-born, feminine principle with its emotionality and instinctiveness reaching far back into the depths of time, and into the roots of physiological continuity. Without a doubt, these concepts are purely intuitive visions, but one cannot dispense with them if one tries to understand the nature of the human soul. China could not dispense with them because, as the history of Chinese philosophy shows, it has never gone so far from central psychic facts as to lose itself in a one-sided over-development and over-valuation of a single psychic function. Therefore, the Chinese have never failed to

Hans Küng, professor of dogmatic and ecumenical theology at the University of Tübingen, Germany

C.G. Jung working on his stone tower in Bolingen on Lake Zurich, 1955:
"Words and paper ... no longer sufficed ... I had to bear witness in stone."

recognize the paradoxes and the polarity inherent in all life. The opposites always balance on the scales – a sign of high culture. One-sidedness, though it lends momentum, is a mark of barbarism. Therefore, I can only take the reaction which begins in the West against the intellect in favour of *eros*, and in favour of intuition, as a mark of cultural advance, a widening of consciousness beyond the too narrow limits set by a tyrannical intellect."[35]

The consciousness of the beyond-the-modern era is characterized by awareness and acceptance of cities' inherent contradictions and complexity. The quest for a good city is in fact much like a game with an infinite number of potential outcomes. Just as with dominoes, soccer or chess, the point is not to achieve control but to develop strategies, to use one's resources sensibly, to seize opportunities when they present themselves, and to develop synergies. The era of simple guidelines, which Blaise Pascal described nearly three hundred years ago as characterized by terrible simpli-fication, of the dictatorship of ultimate visions and plans for cities, and purely hierarchical decision-making, is over. Change or continuity alone are never right or wrong; yet a careful exploration of the energies at work is essential.

Saint Augustine said that he rode his body like his donkey. Modern man has described his city as a *machine à habiter* – a machine for living. He uses its space for housing and working, for streets and parking lots, for sewers and Internet connections much like Saint Augustine used his donkey. And yet our souls long for an entirely different city – one that truly represents communal society in its gestalt, inspired by its living inhabitants. In the beyond-the-modern age, cities could be perceived as part of a greater whole, part of the universe itself. Cities could exist within a conscious rhythm of continuity and trans-formation, of completeness and perfection, of light and dark. Cities would incorporate nature and nature would, in turn, do the same. There could be goals, but not plans.

Near its end, modernism displayed a fascination with newness, a deep-seated need for control, and disdain for the inherent intelligence of cities. Architects were expected to competently create entirely new cities. Unfortunately, this resulted in a fair amount of hubris among architects, an inflated presumption of their own abilities.

The first signs of dissent appeared when the counter-culture revolutionaries of the 1960s rediscovered sociology – a science entirely devoted to studying the needs of human beings. Long trapped within a cultural vacuum, architecture students began questioning the relevance of city gestalt. It was slowly becoming acceptable, once again, to discuss cities from a political and philosophical standpoint and to question the current state of affairs.

Others reacted to the growing cultural and social freedom by hastily seeking new imagery to help placate their growing discomfort with so much change. Led by a British prince, a newfound interest in historicism developed among conservatives who felt alienated by the modern era's radicalism. In the United States, this led to the fulfillment of "the profound American yearning for history."[36] Still others sought answers in deconstructionist theories developed by French philosophers. Romantics, having been without a home for many years, found themselves once more able to translate their feelings into neo-regionalist gestalt. Throughout the world, clever individuals blended all these efforts into an often-pornographic collage of styles.

Unfortunately, much of this energy of change was interpreted as a passing aberration rather than the symptoms of the beginnings of a new era. Architectural theory, especially within those schools where urbanism had been ignored for decades, quickly returned to its sterile modernist roots. Essentially, architects began to behave as though nothing happened. Postmodernism became an evil spirit. I am convinced this is incorrect. What we are witnessing are merely the first clumsy steps of a new era. As early as 1970, philosopher and social critic Theodor W. Adorno wrote: "When impulse can no longer find preestablished security in forms or content," artists "are objectively compelled to experiment."[37]

LEARNING FROM
LAS VEGAS... AND OTHERS

On a somewhat playful level, I named this book *Learning from China* as homage to Robert Venturi, Stephen Izenour, and Denise Scott Brown's *Learning from Las Vegas*, which launched major discourse about beyond-the-modern cities. But on a more personal level, the title refers to my exploration of Chinese Taoist philosophy. Inwardly, my search began many years ago upon reading Alan Watts' *Tao: The Watercourse Way*. Outwardly, it took the form of a prolonged collaboration between myself, as a consulting city planner, and the Chinese city of Kunming. I became aware of the fascinating connection between the theory and practice of Taoism and the major themes of cities in the beyond-the-modern age.

"Passing through Las Vegas is Route 91, the archetype of the commercial strip, the phenomenon at its purest and most intense. We believe a careful documentation and analysis of its physical form is as important to architects and urbanists today as were the studies of medieval Europe and ancient Rome and Greece to earlier generations. Such a study will help to define a new type of urban form emerging in America and Europe, radically different from that we have known; one that we have been ill-equipped to deal with and that, from ignorance, we define today as urban sprawl." [41]

Learning from Las Vegas, which documented a new type of city, was first published in 1972 by the Massachusetts Institute of Technology. It dealt with the Las Vegas Strip and told of "ducks" and the "decorated shed." It questioned the sanctity of modernist dogma and its application in architecture and urban design. As an architecture student in the former East German city of Leipzig, urban planner Iris Reuther told me once that *Learning from Las Vegas* was locked up in a special cabinet along with other forbidden revolutionary books. In order to read it, students needed written authorization from a professor.

Venturi's first book, *Complexity and Contradiction in Architecture*, published in 1966, already drew attention to the oversimplifications of modernism: "Architects can no longer afford to be intimidated by the puritanically modern language of orthodox modern architecture. I like elements that are hybrid rather than 'pure,' compromising rather than 'clean,' distorted rather than 'straightforward,' ... I am for a messy vitality over obvious unity ... I am for richness of meaning rather than clarity of meaning." [42]

From *Learning from Las Vegas* [38] to *The Watercourse Way* [39]. And then on to *The Kunming Project* [40] and back again.

I first heard the expression *terrible simplificateur*, coined in the seventeenth century by French naturalist and religious philosopher Blaise Pascal, from my high school French teacher. It stayed with me to this day. We have tried for millennia to overcome the innate complexities and contradictions of the world. Unfortunately, this drive finally led to an overabundance of so-called terrible simplifications. Finally, in the beyond-the-modern

The Strip...

...the duck and the decorated shed

age, we are beginning to learn how to deal with the contradictions and complexities of our world, and also of our cities, on a new and more sophisticated level.

The major themes of this era also accompanied my personal life. I grew up in a time of terrible simplifications. World War II was the backdrop of my early childhood, the Cold War was in effect during my time as a student and modernism incited glorification rather than debate. The cultural counter-revolution was still far away. As a doctor, my father explained to us children that vitamin shots were far better for our health than vast amounts of salad and vegetables could ever be. The longest hours of my life were spent sitting through Protestant church services – a mandatory part of my confirmation lessons. The explanations and commentaries about my culture's religion were infinitely foreign to me.

I completed my architectural studies in 1960 and designed a technical museum as my diploma project. Central to my design was the flexibility and expandability of each section within the museum. My project lacked any formal connection to a given site, was intensely rational, and allowed for unlimited growth and continuous change. I didn't envision constructing the museum, but rather assembling and disassembling it like a piece of machinery. Architects Renzo Piano and Richard Rogers would later create a similar project in Paris.

My diploma project, a design for a technology museum, 1960

Renzo Piano and Richard Rogers' Centre Pompidou, Paris, 1971

My first job as an architect was with a firm contracted to build the Carouge Towers near Geneva. Four monumental cubes – like huge spacecraft ready for take-off at any time – were built along the axis of the city's historical center. I was fascinated with the concept of simplification. It made my life easier. But it also engendered a growing skepticism within me. Skepticism is sinful when it leads to a loss of faith. Conversely, it is a virtue when it leads to critical awareness in the Taoist sense, when it concerns opening to new things, finding one's own way, and not accepting ideas merely because they are familiar.

At one of the final lectures I attended during my architectural studies, Peter Meyer, a professor of modern art history at the Swiss Federal Institute of Technology in Zurich, mentioned a position in Cairo at the Swiss Institute for Studies in Ancient Egyptian Architecture. The institute was a foundation dedicated to the study of Ancient Egyptian monuments and was mandated to employ only architects. I felt immediately convinced that this offer was meant for me.

Before long, I was on board a ship to Alexandria. Upon arriving in Athens, I decided to interrupt my journey for a week so as to experience the foundations of everything I had studied up until that point. On my very first morning, I saw the Acropolis, walked through the Propylaeum, past the Caryatides, and to the Parthenon. Everything seemed to fit just

Carouge Towers, Geneva, 1956–1960

right. I felt I was witnessing everything I had been taught. "Architecture is the artful, correct and grandiose play of buildings bathed in light ... Egyptian, Greek or Roman architecture is the art of building with prisms, cubes and cylinders, tetrahedrons or spheres: the pyramids, the temple of Luxor, the Parthenon, the Colosseum, Hadrian's Villa ... We must aim at the fixing of standards in order to face the problem of perfection. The Parthenon is a product of selection applied to a standard." [43] In my mind, these great structures were an overwhelming and convincing manifestation of the power of modernism. The Parthenon confirmed all modernist maxims: rigour in the treatment of proportions; uniformity of language; dominance of function; and the supremacy of detached bodies.

Following this climactic experience, my journey took me to an entirely different world. I was part of a team made up of members of the University of Chicago's Oriental Institute and Switzerland's Institute for Studies in Ancient Egyptian Architecture. Egypt's new Aswan Dam was on the verge of flooding five hundred kilometers of the Nile valley and we were participating in the UNESCO campaign to save ancient Nubian monuments. The entire region had to be explored for unfound objects and the valuable monuments had to be inventoried and dismantled.

I became fascinated with modernism's obsessive focus on the physical aspects of structures. Although we spent millions of dollars documenting the past, it was a highly selective process in which a specific version of the past was chosen while others were ruthlessly erased. During the construction of the first Aswan Dam, for instance, a Coptic church, which had at one time been integrated into one of the temples we were studying near Bab Kalabsha, was completely destroyed. The rationale behind this singular decision was that the older seemingly more valuable temple built by Ramses II needed to be isolated so that it could be experienced in all its purity.

The sacred mountain of modernism, drawn by Le Corbusier in 1911

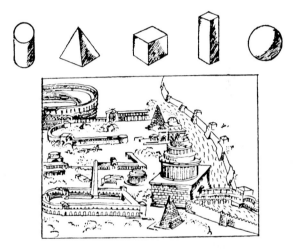

"Architecture is the masterful, correct and magnificent play of masses brought together in light." Le Corbusier, 1922 [44]

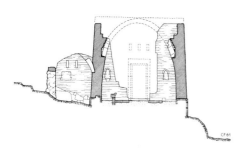

Inventory drawing of a temple in Bêt el Wali, Nubia, Egypt, 1960

The mosque in the village of Hussein Kulek, Nubia, Egypt

No documentation remains concerning this act. Only minute traces of ancient vault joints remained. In retrospect, I should have been documenting the remaining Nubian villages which were completely destroyed by the flood. Instead, I made it my business to try to reconstruct the Coptic Church. Charismatic Egyptian architect Hassan Fathy would later describe the remaining Nubian villages in rapturous terms: "It was a new world for all of us, entire villages with spacious, very beautiful, clean and harmonious houses. In Egypt there was nothing to compare to them. Each village seemed to have been built in a dreamland. Its architecture might have been invented in Atlantis itself." [45]

That period of my life was strongly influenced by the negative side of the female energies of modernism. The negative side of male energy was to destroy everything that was old in order to create space for a new, idealized city. The feminine aspect of modernism, on the other hand, opposed destruction of any kind because it brought about change. In this sense, radical monument preservation is an equally aggressive expression of modernism. It seemed to me at the time that our work on Nubian monuments merely represented a shift, within the same worldview, from one extreme to another. Soon enough, I would have my first encounter with beyond-the-modern urbanism. (Male and female energy are explored further in chapter five.)

Returning from Nubia, I stopped over in Gourna, an ancient village on the hilltops of the west bank of the Nile near Luxor, and spent the night at Sheik Ali Hotel. Perhaps due to his extraordinarily impressive moustache, Sheik Ali Abdel-Rassoul had been cast as the chief of an evil gang of tomb raiders in a major Hollywood motion picture. With his earnings, he bought the abandoned German Archaeological Institute building and transformed it into an inexpensive inn. Sheik Ali – whose grandfather had been involved in one of the largest, and shadiest, discoveries of the Theban necropolis – frequently offered

The old village of Gourna above the necropolises near
the Valley of the Kings

antiquities such as mummy beads and
sarcophagi lids to hotel guests gathered for
communal evening meals. The fictitious role
he had played on film merged seamlessly
with reality.

In the 1950s, at the request of the Egyptian
Department of Antiquities, a city named
New Gourna was built a short distance from
Sheik Ali's inn. The new city was supposed
to accommodate the resettlement of nine
hundred Old-Gourna families. To the dismay
of the Department of Antiquities, it appeared
the villagers had been taking advantage of
their privileged location and plundering
the treasures beneath their homes for great
profit – with Sheik Ali's support no doubt.

New Gourna's urban design was definitely
not characterized by what Le Corbusier had
described as the "artful, correct and grandiose
play of buildings bathed in light." Instead,
Egyptian architect Hassan Fathy conceived it
as an amalgam of North African and Arabian
city planning. It was playfully laid out as
a network of interwoven narrow lanes, town

squares, and building spaces. Built to face
inward, the homes accommodated the local
climate and upheld its residents' specific
societal values. Regional building techniques,
essentially based on the use of dried clay
bricks, dictated both the style and method
used to construct New Gourna. [46]

Fathy had created an inspired city; one perfectly suited to its location, period in time,
and inhabitants. It was a work of genius that
appropriated, reinterpreted, and intelligently
combined traditional forms, structures, and
building techniques. New Gourna's gestalt
evolved out of the needs, goals, and dreams of
its inhabitants as well as a profound respect
for time and place. I was confronted, for the
very first time, with a convincing alternative
truth. It was a relative truth and did not
claim to be absolute.

Learning from Las Vegas did not formulate
a counter-position. Instead, it pointed in
a radically different direction by expanding
the academic debate about the difference,
in reference to cities, between a "modern

New pigeon house in New-Gourna

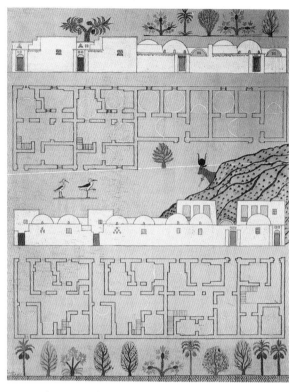

Drawings of New-Gourna by Hassan Fathy, 1948

Street in New-Gourna

duck" and a "postmodern decorated shed."
Stating that "Main Street is almost in order,"
pointed to a different attitude toward caring
for the transformation of cities, one that
did not seek perfection or completeness, but
instead sought to capitalize on the opportunities of time and place. In an afterword
to Venturi's *Complexity and Contradiction in
Architecture*, German architecture critic
Heinrich Klotz synthesized Venturi's theory
thus: "'Mannerism' was defined as a reaction
to 'Classicism,' which countered simplicity
with complexity, the static and fixed with the
labile, the banal with the refined, the easily
understood with lack of clarity, the incon-
testable with contradictoriness, simplicity
with ambiguity." [47]

In this interpretation, Venturi's position is
decidedly Taoist. It also corresponds, in a surprisingly close way, to my own understanding
of our times. I wish therefore to use this
understanding as a guideline for viewing the
world, and the cities, in which we live today.
In the following, when I use the word China,
I am not referring to contemporary China
but to the heritage of the Taoist philosophy
that evolved in China over the course of
two millennia.

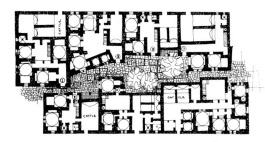

General layout of New-Gourna

Southeastern section of the village square with the "Khan"

Lao-tzu riding on a buffalo

TAO CANNOT BE DEFINED IN WORDS AND IS NOT AN IDEA OR
CONCEPT. THUS THE TAO IS THE COURSE, THE FLOW, THE DRIFT,
OR THE PROCESS OF NATURE. THE PERSON WHO LIVES IN TAO
UNDERSTANDS THE POLARITY AND THE INNER UNITY OF YIN AND
YANG, THE FEMININE AND THE MASCULINE PRINCIPLE, HE KNOWS
THE WISDOM OF ACTING WITHOUT VIOLENCE, HE FOLLOWS THE
'WATERCOURSE WAY,' BECAUSE EVERYTHING IN LIFE IS FLUID.
WITHOUT DECAY, THERE IS NO GROWTH, WITHOUT DEATH NO LIFE
AND WITHOUT PAIN NO JOY.

— *Allan Watts* [48]

LEARNING FROM CHINA
AND THE WATERCOURSE WAY

Alan Watts' introduction to Taoism, *Tao: The Watercourse Way*, was published posthumously in 1975. Two decades later, François Jullien, a Chinese philosophy and literature professor at the University of Paris VII, noted that from the Chinese perspective, knowledge and action are not two seperate issues. There is but one concern and it encompasses both the way of things and their use. The Chinese have summarized this in a single term: Tao.

Taoism strives to adapt to the rhythms of the universe and the order of natural law. Neither lawmaker nor creator regulates metaphysical space. Each individual element has its place in the cosmos. Remarkably, elements and principles of Western science – like holograms, morphogenic fields, and synchronicity – are in synch with this worldview. The spiritual practices and lifestyle of those who consciously live in the beyond-the-modern era are also in agreement with this perspective.

Tao: The Watercourse Way defines four axioms: the principle of polarity; the principle of cyclicity; the principle of mindfulness; and the principle of unity between man and nature.

Polarity implies not only that the world consists of polar systems, but also that polar opposites are necessary and complementary to one another. Nature, for instance, functions through the interplay of apparent opposites: humidity and dryness, warmth and cold, brightness and darkness, male and female. Rather than independent opposites, the Taoist polarities of *yin* and *yang* are in fact continuously renewing and interweaving forces within the universe.

In Taoist philosophy, the world is referred to as *tiandi*, meaning heaven and earth. The human head, with its round shape, is compared to heaven and human feet, with their rectangular shape, are compared to earth. Heaven embodies the masculine and the mind, earth represents the feminine and the material. Thus, understanding the world becomes a matter of realizing that those who are driven by the mind may be no different than those driven by materialistic behavior. This is expressed in the famous Taoist saying: "Heaven and earth are father and mother of the ten thousand things."

Taoism does not draw a distinction between body and soul. Instead, humankind is perceived as a continuum of *chi*, of uninterrupted energy or *pneuma*, the vital spirit. The concept of soul as a purely spiritual entity, distinct from the physical body, is foreign to Taoist thought. In the cosmic realm, men and women are a microcosm of *xing*, the character or nature of heaven and earth. From earth, humankind receives its blood, or what Westerners would call body, and from heaven, it receives breath, or soul.

Taoist philosopher He Shang-gong described the relationship thus: "[In the beginning,] the Way gave birth to the One. The One gave birth to the Two: it created Yin and Yang. The Two gave birth to the Three: Yin and Yang create the harmonious, the clear and the clouded, the three breaths, which are divided into Heaven, Earth and Man. The Three gave birth to creations: Heaven, Earth and Man together create everything. The Heaven spreads, the Earth transforms, and Man educates and nourishes." [50]

The Taoist worldview of the cosmos as living organism is difficult for modern Western man to assimilate. We are so accustomed to viewing the physical world as separate from ourselves and hostile, or as purely material, that the Taoist view of a unified universe is completely foreign. Humankind is part of this unity, part of heaven and earth. It forms a single body and a single experience. This is the central thesis of Taoist thought. It concerns itself with humankind as a reflection of the cosmos. There is no single god, creator and ruler of humankind and the cosmos. In Chinese philosophy, there is no such separation between man and god.

British scholar and scientist Joseph Needham devoted much of his life's work to exploring Chinese history. In *Science and Civilization in China*, first published in 1954, Needham explored the fundamental differences in the Chinese worldview. "While Greek thought as a whole moved ... towards concepts of mechanical cause and effect, Chinese thought developed the organic concept. It is a mistake, and a serious one, to think of this Chinese outlook on Nature as essentially primitive. It was a precisely ordered universe, not governed either by the fiat of a supreme creator-lawgiver nor by the inexorable clashes of atoms, but by a harmony of wills, spontaneous but ordered in patterns, rather like the dancers in a country dance, none of whom are bound by law or pushed by the others, but who cooperate voluntarily." [51]

German philosopher, physicist, and mathematician Gottfried Leibniz studied the Taoist worldview with great intensity. His theory about monads, published in 1714, was strongly influenced by twelfth-century Chinese thinking. After reading texts provided to him by Jesuit missionaries living in China, Leibniz became so overwhelmed that he immediately

wrote Czar Peter the Great. "In my view, the state of our affairs is such that I...believe it necessary that Chinese missionaries should be sent to us." [52] Leibniz was the first, according to Needham, to "bridge the chasm between the idealism of theology and the materialism of European science." [53]

In 1929, psychoanalyst Carl Jung also addressed the subject. He had been asked to pen a foreword to Richard Wilhelm's translation of *The Secret of the Golden Flower: A Chinese Book of Life*, an esoteric Chinese text first published in the eighteenth century. *The Secret of the Golden Flower* explained how people could reach "a state of the psyche lifting them above all the misery of life" [54] through the cultivation and guidance of psychic and alchemical energies. Wilhelm, who lived as a pastor in the German-built Chinese port of Jiaozhou (formerly Tsingtau) between 1899 and 1921, had undertaken the first comprehensive translation of the *I Ching*, "the book of wisdom that has permeated all Chinese thought for millennia." [55] In his foreword, Jung acknowledges the "Tao as a method or conscious way to unify that which is separate ... The great difficulty in interpreting this and similar texts for the European mind is due to the fact that the Chinese author always starts from the centre of things, from the point we would call his objective or goal; in a word, he begins with the ultimate insight he has set out to attain. Thus the Chinese author begins his work with ideas that demand a most comprehensive understanding on our part. So much so, that a man with a critical intellect feels he speaks with laughable pretension, or even that he is guilty of utter nonsense, if he dares launch a purely intellectual discourse on the subtle psychic experiences of the great minds of the East. For example, our text begins: 'That which exists through itself, is called Tao.' ... It is characteristic of the Western mind that it has no concept for Tao." [56]

In Wilhelm's text, the word Tao was translated as "meaning." Others translated it as "the way" and "providence." The Jesuits equated its meaning with the word God. The symbol for Tao combines the Chinese ideograms for head and walking. The former likely refers to consciousness, the latter to traveling a path. Combined, this reflects "walking consciously," or "the conscious way." [57]

For Jung, the search for consciousness seemed linked to the divergence between "the idealism of theology and the materialism of European science." In his foreword to *The Secret of the Golden Flower*, he expresses skepticism about whether Western man can cope with bridging this chasm. He notes that it is "better for Western man not to know too much of the secret insights of the Eastern sage at first, for it would be the right tool in the hand of the wrong man." In the conclusion to his foreword, however, he appears to have overcome his reservations: "Western consciousness is by no means consciousness in general, but rather a historically conditioned, and geographically limited, factor, representative of only one part of humanity. The widening of our consciousness ought not to proceed at the expense of other kinds of consciousness, but ought to take place through the development of those elements of our psyche which are analogous to those of a foreign psyche ... The European invasion of the East was a deed of violence on a great scale, and it has left us the duty ... of understanding the mind of the East. This is perhaps more necessary than we realize at present." [58]

Later in his work, Needham concluded that as modern science goes beyond a Newtonian understanding of the universe, it must incorporate Taoist perspective into the equation in order to arrive at a balanced worldview. This, I believe, applies equally to our care of cities.

In caring for our cities, it is implied that there is intercourse, or interaction, with those we are charged with caring for. This implies a connection with another, or the other. Caring, however, can be interpreted in many ways. In caring for another, I may regard this other as a soulless object, no different than the stones I kick out of my path, or use to construct my house. The city I construct, in this case, is really no more than a heap of assembled rocks, utterly unrelated to me.

Conversely, I can view caring for another as caring for a part of the universe that is indelibly linked to myself. In this instance, despite this connection, I may still view the other as an underdog whose existence impedes my progress. The city thus becomes the whore of Babylon, the embodiment of all things threatening. I must rule it or escape it.

Alternately, I may choose to worship the other as a great deity, overpoweringly spiritual, who manifests itself every few millennia. On this level, the city becomes a holy Jerusalem, the utopia we will never attain in our sinful states.

Finally, I may also regard the other as my friend. We take care of one another in a physical, emotional, and spiritual manner. On this level – a Taoist perspective – I become part of the city and it of me. This worldview is just now being rediscovered in Western thought after modernism squashed it from our consciousness. It just barely survived among esoteric Western practices such as astrology, cabala, tarot, alchemy, and geomancy. Thus the case for caring for our cities could just as well be made through an exploration of Western esoteric practice and its proponents. Throughout history, there have been Western thinkers who drew on this worldview, including Paracelsus, Goethe, and Rudolf Steiner. Later, Albert Einstein, Carl Jung, and Werner Heisenberg took up the torch. And in the beyond-the-modern age, it is thinkers such as Wolfgang Welsch, Rupert Sheldrake, and

Ken Wilber. Taoism is a worldview based on the unity of humankind and the universe – the Tao – which leads to a corresponding system of ethics – the *te*. By achieving an understanding of the self as it relates to the cosmos, the individual becomes part of the great cosmic game. Our job is to play the game well. A set of principles serve to guide us along the path: the principle of harmony, as expressed through *yin* and *yang*; of mindfulness, as expressed through *wu wei*; and of respect, as expressed through *feng shui*.

In the following I shall attempt, as Alan Watts wrote, "to show how the principle of the Tao reconciles sociability with individuality, order with spontaneity, and unity with diversity." [59]

The tenets of Taoist philosophy present a strong lens through which to view and understand caring for our cities and the predominant themes of the beyond-the-modern era. The following concepts also correspond to the chapter divisions within Alan Watts' *Tao: The Watercourse Way*, with the exception of my addition of a chapter about *feng shui*. Thus, beyond-the-modern urbanism, the Tao of the city, incorporates the following six premises:

Tao:
All aspects of humankind, not just its
rationality, should be considered in urbanism.

Symbolism:
A city's gestalt – its structure, form, and
symbols – always reflects meaning. The more
intensive the gestalt's aesthetic, the greater
the city's strength.

Yin and Yang:
Caring for the continuous transformation
of cities must never become a war of truths,
ideologies, or dogmas. It should be undertaken
as a game of balancing less with more, too
little with too much.

無爲

Wu Wei:
The central task of the urbanist is to oversee
this game mindfully and without prejudice.

風水

Feng Shui:
Consciousness of man's harmony with the
universe should be integrated into the gestalt
of the city.

Te:
If the aforementioned five concepts are taken
seriously, the culture and politics of urbanism
will become enriched and the urbanist's profession as a whole will become infused with
fresh energy and new challenges.

Ghardaia, Algeria

———

THE TAO IS THAT FROM WHICH ONE CANNOT DEVIATE; THAT FROM
WHICH ONE CAN DEVIATE IS NOT THE TAO.

— *From 'The Doctrine of the Mean,' quoted by Alan Watts* [60]

PREMISE:
ALL ASPECTS OF HUMANKIND,
NOT JUST ITS RATIONALITY, SHOULD
BE CONSIDERED IN URBANISM.

Carl Jung devoted substantial study to the potentials of the human mind. He began by making the distinction between thought and intuition. Rational thought helps us deal with the outside material world. We need it to decipher and make sense of how the cities, and the world we live in, ultimately work. Intuition and spirituality provide access to an inner world – both our own and that of the collective, cosmic realm – where we can tap into ideas that go beyond the physical. These ideas contain information about what the French call *l'outre monde*. Without access to

these intuitions, we become mere observers, passengers traveling through this world. As such, we are victims of a hostile world that we may only experience on a physical level. Intuition, anchored in the soul, allows us to see ourselves as intricate parts of the universe, participants in the great game of the cosmos.

We experience the physical world with our senses. Our emotions, on the other hand, help us process this information into experiences of beauty or repulsion, intensity or banality, joy or fear. Thought and intuition are therefore linked through feeling and sensing.

A renewed interest in the integration of disparate parts, of healing separation, is becoming apparent today throughout various fields of study. Cities must also participate in this quest. The word Tao is often translated as "the way." The Tao of the city is this quest, the quest for integration.

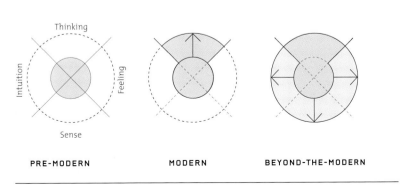

PRE-MODERN   MODERN   BEYOND-THE-MODERN

The evolution of human consciousness from the pre-modern to the beyond-the-modern era

CONSCIOUS INTERACTION WITH RATIONALITY

Modernism made exploring rationality, and its effect on all fields of knowledge, its central focus. Other aspects of the human mind, such as those manifested in spirituality and art, were neglected and discriminated against. Critics of modernism often point to the hostile polarities of rationality and spirituality. Scientific thought, the offspring of rigorous rationality, becomes the scapegoat for a civilization gone astray and for the despicable cities it built in the process. Seeking support for anti-rationality, Westerners often turn to Buddhism. But in so doing, Buddhism is taken out of its cultural context and reduced to a one-dimensional escape route that leaves rational thought behind in favor of over-dependence on intuition, feeling, and sensing.

Taoism teaches us that while scientific thought is indispensable, it must always remain in balance with emotion, sensory perception, and intuition. The error of modern rationality is the radical nature of its ambition and, consequently, its disdain for all other aspects of human existence. Our ability to think and explore the physical world need not be fundamentally brought into question; instead, it should be consciously brought into balance with the many other aspects of our being. We must relearn how to trust and cultivate our senses, how to take our feelings seriously. This polarity does not insist on opposites, where too much of one threatens the other. Instead, it requires the development of equal parts, of the delicate balance between the many aspects of human potential.

Using the city as illustration, this doesn't mean we must rip our sewers from the ground and tear our satellites from the heavens. It does mean that we must begin providing the city with sensual, emotional, and spiritual qualities to balance out its intense rationality. This will allow the city to grow from a machine-like state into a collective vessel for our souls.

REINTEGRATION OF EMØTION AND SENSUALITY

The guiding principle of modern design theory was that form follows function. This meant that science-obsessed modernists strove to elevate faith in technology and rationality to dogmatic levels. It was believed that each article of human invention, from teapots to skyscrapers, should illustrate this belief. Today, form follows function has lost its verve and cities are no longer temples of rationality. Besides rationality, people now look to cities to find the other missing traces of their existence as well.

Hans Küng described the values of the beyond-the-modern age as imagination, sensitivity, emotion, warmth, tenderness, and humanity. All these are linked to the human potential for emotion. A vast vocabulary defines the rational domain, but everyday language that effectively deals with our capacity for emotion is severely impoverished. The Swiss-German dialect, for instance, lacks an adequate translation for "I love you." The most heartfelt declaration of love a Swiss person can utter is "Ich ha di gärn," which means "I like you." Even as I write these words about emotion, they seem barren to me, colored by a hangover from my Zurich heritage in the Protestant faith of the late Middle Ages.

The job of reintegrating emotion and sensuality into the gestalt of our cities is a big one, and after decades of being discriminated against, one whose importance is only now beginning to emerge in public discourse. As a highly visual culture, especially in film, but also in architecture and urban design, we now find ourselves inundated with vulgar – or what I call pornographic – imagery. Naturally, elitist architecture provides a few exceptions, but I am referring here to a saturation of vulgar buildings and infrastructure and how we deal with that saturation. In this context, sensuality and emotion are expressed in their coarsest forms because their transformation into refinement is still not taken seriously.

The phenomenal success of Austrian artist Friedensreich Hundertwasser, a celebrated painter and architect in German-speaking countries, is a perfect example. His interest in transforming superficial sensuality into concrete form had broad popular appeal and was both compelling and difficult to ignore. Yet what in his paintings appeared like poetry, in his buildings became transformed into a vulgar and purely decorative style. Clearly, his widespread success occurred because he was filling a distinct sensual void.

Transforming energy on a higher plane is the essence of all our endeavors. Sexual lust, for instance, should not lead to pornography but to eroticism. Male energy should be transformed into creativity instead of aggression. Female energy should be infused into caring for that which is precious rather than being transformed into obsessive desire for control and fear of change. Reintegrating these neglected and sublimating aspects of humankind is one of the great challenges of the beyond-the-modern age. But how can Küng's "imagination, sensibility, warmth, tenderness, and humanity" be translated into concrete form? By way of illustration, I will present three architectural examples: the integration of a new building into a city, the conversion of an old house, and the construction of a solitary structure in a mountain valley.

The pilgrimage chapel at Ronchamp, France, designed by Le Corbusier, 1950–54

Prefabricated housing near Zurich, built around 1960

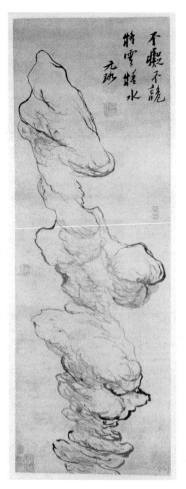

不癡不詭
幻雲幻水
元璐

Ni Yunlu, clouds-water-stone, seventeenth century.
Material and simultaneously an expression of
animated immateriality. The inscription on the top
right corner reads: "Not insane, not simulated;
perhaps clouds, perhaps water."

DESIGNING A BUILDING FOR BASEL'S HEBELSTRASSE 11

The first example concerns a project designed
by internationally renowned Basel-based
Swiss architects Herzog & de Meuron. The
catalogue for Herzog & de Meuron's 2002
exhibit at the Canadian Center for Architecture contains a fascinating link to this book's
subject. After writing in some depth about
Chinese scholar stones, author Albert Lutz
notes that it is in fact, "neither these stones
nor the high points of Chinese architecture
that concern us here. Instead, it is the vocabulary and stories created by Chinese artists and
men of letters through their contemplation
of stone – a particularly fascinating subject
in the context of Herzog & de Meuron's work.
The world of Chinese scholar stones, mysteriously shrouded in feathery mist, is a source
of inspiration to anyone interested in transparency, transformation, the immaterial,
dynamism, spectacular surfaces, monoliths,
raw lumps of rock, and minimalist and
archaic monuments." [61]

In 1984, Herzog & de Meuron won the architectural competition I had organized to
design a building that would fill a courtyard
space on Hebelstrasse in the historic section
of Basel. Just as Lutz would describe their work
nearly a decade later, they created a building
characterized by, "transparency, transformation, the immaterial, dynamism, and spectacular surfaces." While integrated into the
old town structure, the building was, in Lutz's
words, also a monolith and a minimalist or
archaic monument.

Jacques Herzog and his family moved into
one of the building's top-floor apartments
in 1988 where they still live today. The building
appears like a "wooden box that floats above
the ground with a sophisticated lightness" [62]
and is, in my view, an exemplary symbol
of how different the beyond-the-modern city
can be: sensual, without being coarse, diversified and complex without abandoning order,
tender and yet robust, autonomous but
nevertheless respectful of its surroundings,
creating identity without currying favor.

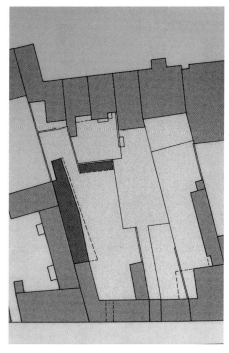

General layout Hebelstrasse, Basel

View from courtyard in the direction of the Hebelstrasse

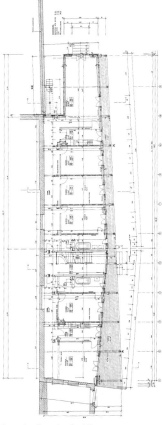

Floor plan for 2nd and 3rd floors

REHABILITATING BASEL'S SPALENBERG 12

The spatial sequence created by Spanish architect Santiago Calatrava in the existing historic Spalenhof building radiates a completely different aesthetic than the Hebelstrasse project. The purpose of the project was to provide access, within the Spalenhof building, to two small theaters. The centerpiece of the restoration is a complex load-bearing structure into which a staircase is integrated. It is a design deeply imbued with imagination. Visitors are overwhelmed by the structure's elegance and dynamic energy. At the same time, Calatrava deftly creates a stark contrast between his design and the existing historical structure.

The landmark-protected Spalenhof is one of the most important secular public monuments in the city of Basel. Its Romanesque interior structure was first referenced in 1247 and German emperor Ferdinand I was received in its large hall in 1563. The breakthrough in the project's challenging development process came only once we involved Calatrava. He integrated technology, art, and philosophy into a comprehensive design. As in nearly all his projects, he ingeniously transformed a technical task into a highly sophisticated gestalt.

Entrance to the Spalenhof

The two-story, load-bearing structure in the renovated building that integrates a staircase to the upper theatre

REDEVELOPING A THERMAL SPA IN VALS

The first example, the Hebelstrasse project, is one of the most beautiful I know of; the second example, the Spalentor spatial sequence, is one of the most surprising; but certainly the most sensual creation I have witnessed is Swiss architect Peter Zumthor's design for a thermal spa in Switzerland's remote Alpine village of Vals.

The thermal baths themselves are the central sensual experience. Through their careful and intricate design, visitors embark on a journey of sensuality. Hot water, cold water; dry air, humid air; dark rooms, bright rooms; rough stones, smooth stones; quiet spaces, resounding spaces; narrow views, expansive views; introverted situations, extroverted situations. The sequence and order of the spaces, their transitions and differing characteristics, clearly add to the richness of this unique experience. Should Fellini have had the opportunity to visit this spa, he would surely have wanted to shoot a film here. I find the economic impact of the thermal springs equally remarkable. Zumthor's project replaced a horrid 1960s bathhouse and spa complex which had declared bankruptcy, no doubt due in part to its unattractive design. The new spa, fresh and invigorating, created a dramatic increase in the number of visitors to Vals. In fact, the spa is finally financially successful and contributes considerably to the valley's economic stability. Beauty and aesthetics, it seems, are crucial elements toward creating economic viability. I believe investors are once again beginning to believe this in the beyond-the-modern age.

Upon completing a draft of this book, I asked my good friend Iris Reuther, a town planner in Leipzig, Germany, to read it and provide commentary. Two weeks later I received this postcard from her:
"Dear Carl: We spent a wonderful Saturday in Vals and I began to have an even better sense of what is meant by the notion of integrating spirituality with good architecture in the right location. In short, urbanism at its best."

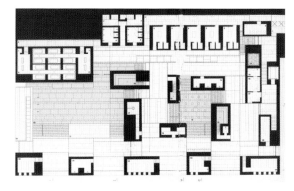

Floor plan of pool level

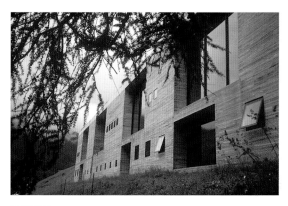

East facade

The large indoor pool

POTENTIAL

"The age of Socratic man is past: crown yourselves with ivy, grasp the thyrsus and do not be amazed if tigers and panthers lie down fawning at your feet. Now dare to be tragic men, for you will be redeemed. You shall join the Dionysiac procession from India to Greece! Gird yourselves for a hard battle, but have faith in the miracles of your god!"
Friedrich Nietzsche [63]

In the sensual domain, important new themes are emerging that supercede mere trends in the beyond-the-modern age. Because I am referring here primarily to our expanding potential for sensual experience, perhaps the adjective "new" isn't entirely appropriate. We expand and deepen our consciousness of the world by utilizing our sensory organs to see, smell, taste, hear, and feel more intensely and carefully. The eye is our most active sensory organ, the one we depend on the most. Light, experienced as color, and contrast between light and dark, is therefore where our search for new experiences is the most pronounced. Deepening these experiences of sensory perception, therefore, is where we are encountering new experiences. These new experiences essentially concern ranges between too much and too little; the desire for exposure or the need for protection; the pornographic versus the aesthetic. The following examples might shed further light on this.

The artificial cloud at Swiss EXPO 02 in Yverdon

Experiencing Color

I live in a middle-class Zurich neighborhood
that is dominated by mostly post-World War
II houses painted in delightful nuances of
light-gray and off-white. In designing the
three-building apartment complex in which
I live, Annette Gigon and Mike Guyer, two
architects from the Swiss firm Gigon/Guyer,
decided to paint each building in a contrasting
bright color. Benedikt Loderer, the editor of
Swiss architectural magazine *Hochparterre*,
dramatically claimed in the magazine's June
22, 2003 issue that "Everyone is outraged at
the preposterous mustard ochre, dove gray
and lemon yellow." During the design phase
of the project, artist Adrian Schiess had pushed
for painting one of the facades crimson but
the client, a protestant women's association,
had refused based on the assumption that
crimson was clearly a "Catholic" color. Nevertheless, the women's association daringly
approved a bright color scheme for their development – impossible in Zurich only a few
years earlier. I believe this is a small intimation
of some of the untapped potential for
expanded sensual experiences in our time.

Loderer, the editor, disagreed, claiming
that colorful expression was but a backward-
looking trend and a remnant of modernist
tradition. After all, German architect Bruno
Taut painted his Magdeburg houses like Easter
eggs and Le Corbusier was a major proponent
of multi-colored architecture. While in various
instances this may indeed be true, it fundamentally contradicts the thesis of this book.
What we are witnessing today is not a con-
tinuation of elitist classic modernism, instead,
after an annoying postmodernist intermezzo,
I believe we are in reality now witnessing
symptoms of the beyond-the-modern age.

The three-building apartment complex on
Zurich's Susenbergstrasse, designed by Gigon/Guyer

Expansion of Scherr school complex in Zurich, designed
by architect Patrick Gmür, wall created by Peter Roesch, 2002
"Introducing color in architecture goes beyond what is
familiar and accepted. In this 'All over,' the color field not only
loses its frame of reference, but spaces themselves seem to
dissolve. We may thus ask two questions: Is that which seems
to dissolve in the energy field of colors still architecture?
Is that which is adapted by architecture as color material still
considered painting? One could say that both disciplines
reveal what is essential." [64]

Los Angeles, 1959

Controlling light at my Susenbergstrasse
apartment in Zurich

Experiencing Light

One of modernism's great simplifications
dealt with the "stereotypical over-exposure to
light through endless windows," as art histo-
rian Adolf Vogt recently wrote in the *Neue
Zürcher Zeitung*. [65] Large expanses of glass
replaced windows and fluorescent lighting
created a bright, shadow-free work environment. In my new Zurich apartment, I had
to resort to placing wall-to-wall bookshelves
in front of some of its vast windows to protect myself from the overwhelming light.

Once again, new sensibilities and differentiations are emerging which are important
to the gestalt of the city. Nowadays, city
authorities try to create identity for a project
or site through carefully designed lighting.
Artists such as James Turrel are hired to invest
buildings with specific aesthetic qualities
through the medium of light.

Nocturnal lighting on Zurich's Limmat river

The Tower of Winds in Yokahama by Toyo Ito

Light installation by James Turrell for Austria's Kunsthaus Bregenz, 1997

"The Ruhr: a region where industry joins culture." [66]

Experiencing Touch

In an article titled *Towards a Critical Regionalism*, architect and critic Kenneth Frampton writes that the sense of touch is used to "balance the priority accorded the image and to counter the Western tendency to interpret the environment in exclusively perspectival terms. According to its etymology, perspective means rationalized sight or clear seeing, and as such it presupposes a conscious suppression of the senses of smell, hearing, and taste, and a consequent distancing from a more direct experience of the environment ... The tactile and the tectonic jointly have the capacity to transcend the mere appearance of the technical in much the same way as the place-form has the potential to withstand the relentless onslaught of global modernization." [67]

Experiencing Smell

At an exhibit called Alpine Scents, visitors got the chance to take in Switzerland on an olfactory level. A review in the local newspaper described the experience thus: "Daphne, cowherd's sweat, resin, lynx droppings, Kafi schnapps, consecrated oil, funicular grease, and mountain hay." Visitors inhaled "a kind of cultural history of the alpine region ... nothing can awaken more intensive memories than the sense of smell – as everyone knows ever since Marcel Proust's novel *A la Recherche du Temps Perdu*." [68]

Experiencing Sound

For years, Swiss architect Pascal Amphoux, whom I met through a research program organized by the Swiss National Fund, [69] worked at recording and describing the quality and identity of urban soundscapes. He deals with the world of sound beyond the purely defensive approach of our time where sound is often interpreted as noise. Like so many other currently emerging areas of experimentation, it seems to me that this one offers an extraordinary number of undiscovered sensory potentials.

REINTEGRATING SPIRITUALITY

Reintegrating spirituality into human consciousness is the most complex and challenging task of the beyond-the-modern age. It requires reconnecting to the transpersonal and the divine, as well as reintegrating body, soul, and spirit. It is also about a relationship to physical space – the city, in this case – as a point of reference for humankind's anchoring in the cosmos.

I find the work of philosopher and author Ken Wilber very helpful in this context. In *No Boundary: Eastern and Western Approaches to Personal Growth*, published in 1979, Wilber writes about the human tendency to alienate itself from spirituality and suggests solutions for breaking down these boundaries. Modern man, he writes, rejected his ability to be embedded, or rooted, in the cosmos. As a matter of habit, we constantly set up divisions between rational and spiritual consciousness, between consciousness and the body, be-

tween the self and the outside environment. Boundaries are exclusionary. They impart judgment on what is familiar and foreign, safe and threatening, good and evil. [70]

Society's profound need for reintegrating spirituality – increasingly apparent in religion, philosophy, medicine, psychology, physics, and also urbanism – cries out for the dismantling of these boundaries. At issue is our self-awareness as spiritual beings, our intuition that we belong to something greater and that we must find our place on earth, in the cosmos, or in a divine universe. Carl Jung, Teilhard de Chardin [71], Rupert Sheldrake [72], Stanislav Grof [73], and many others write about this at length.

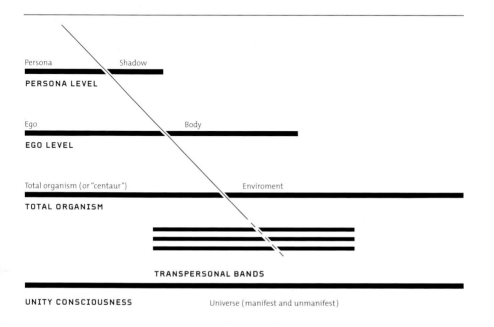

Persona   Shadow
PERSONA LEVEL

Ego   Body
EGO LEVEL

Total organism (or "centaur")   Enviroment
TOTAL ORGANISM

TRANSPERSONAL BANDS

UNITY CONSCIOUSNESS   Universe (manifest and unmanifest)

Ken Wilber's spectrum of consciousness

The universe encompasses all things and humankind is just one of the many energetic manifestations within it. As I understand it, our role within the universe is to participate in a collective broadening and deepening of consciousness. In Western ecclesiastic parlance, the transcendental manifestation of this consciousness is called God. This development takes place on a physical, soul, and spiritual level. We call it evolution.

The collective phenomena of the universe are referred to as nature. Through the natural sciences, we have assiduously strived to understand nature's functions. Through physics, we seek to understand the micro- and macrocosm; through biology and chemistry, we seek to comprehend what lies between the micro- and macrocosm. Exploration of our collective souls and spirits, however, has fallen far behind and is just now becoming once more an acceptable pursuit. Terms such as archetypes, morphogenic fields, and the Gaia hypothesis are emerging in the process. Since the 1970s, we have sought access to these dimensions using both old and new methods, including shamanism, hallucinogenic drugs, holotropic breathing, and transpersonal psychology. New discoveries in the natural sciences correspond with explanations of the cosmos from these areas of research. These correspondences are obvious among such widely used terms as energy, polarity, and holarchy.

Although it must soon become an integral part of urbanism, I still see little evidence right now of these discoveries in the theory and practice of caring for cities. I would venture to guess that the substantial energy devoted to studying the so-called technical sciences of ecology and sustainability is in fact intuitively driven by a search for greater meaning and the Western desire to develop spiritual consciousness. Still, because these subjects remain so new and challenging, there is a definite lack of focus and the boundaries between emotion and spirituality remain yet undefined. At the beginning of a new consciousness, the expression of our desire for spiritual integration is primarily manifest on a city's structural plane and less on its formal plane. I explore this further in my discussion of *feng shui* in chapter nine.

Lucca, Italy

—

**AN OFTEN QUOTED CHINESE PROVERB IS THAT ONE PICTURE
IS WORTH A THOUSAND WORDS, BECAUSE IT IS SO OFTEN MUCH
EASIER TO SHOW THAN TO SAY.**

__ *Alan Watts* [74]

SYMBOL

PREMISE:
A CITY'S GESTALT – ITS STRUCTURE,
FORM, AND SYMBOLS – ALWAYS RE-
FLECTS MEANING. THE MORE INTENSE
THE GESTALT'S AESTHETIC, THE
GREATER THE CITY'S STRENGTH.

In the first chapter of *Tao: The Watercourse Way*, Watts writes about the symbolic quality of Chinese script. Since he does not provide a poignant term from the Chinese language to illustrate his point, I must choose my own. In this context, I will use the word symbol as a synonym for gestalt. A symbol is an image that has meaning. In order to convey our thoughts, ideas, and internal imagery to others, we must convert them into language. Language is a linear code. Letters, words, and sentences are placed in sequence to convey a message. Symbols, or images, are based on a different code. Not only do they convey a broad range of information, but that information can be processed on many different levels and within a framework of entirely different themes. This is especially true for Chinese characters. Each character represents an image, which in turn represents one or several other meanings. This accounts for the richness of Chinese script, as well as the challenges one faces in working with it.

The same applies to the city and its parts. The four-dimensionality of cities in space and time, their holarchy and complex layering, allow for multiple interpretations. Even the slightest intervention by an architect or engineer into a city's gestalt is therefore significant. It is an intrusion into a constantly evolving interpretation. Often, the intervention, the new symbol or image, gets lost in the great flood of "the ten thousand things." On occasion, however, it will instigate a so-called tipping point, a decisive shift in the characterization of a space. Among others, I am thinking here of Frank Gehry's Guggenheim Museum in Bilbao, or of the Eiffel Tower. The new symbol will always significantly alter the text.

The World Trade Center was destroyed, according to New York architects Elizabeth Diller and Ricardo Scofidio, creators of the Swiss Expo 02 artificial cloud, "because they were symbols of some good things and some bad things. We must therefore think with greater clarity about the symbolism of our architecture." [75] The fact that the form of things has lost its innocence is a crucial aspect of the beyond-the-modern age. When form was exclusively defined by function, it could be regarded as scientific, neutral, and absolutely correct – innocent, so to speak. But our era has freed itself from these modern simplifications. We must think "with greater clarity about the symbolism" because we are entering unknown symbolic territory. In our dealings with symbols, we are using a new, more complex and deeply encoded language.

The symbolic force of intervening in the city – whether by building new public space, designing a building with a strong identity, laying a new street, planning a new neighborhood, planting a tree, or, conversely, removing an element, a street, a building, or a tree – depends on both the aesthetic quality and symbolic meaning of the new gestalt.

THE SYMBOLIC MEANING OF GESTALT

Across all cultures, the act of building produces a symbolic gestalt. Gottfried Semper, the master of nineteenth-century classic German architecture, noted that, "The individual peculiarities of the different systems of architecture will remain incomprehensible to us until we have gained an understanding of the socio-political and religious conditions of those nations and ages to which the architectural styles in question belonged. Architectural monuments are indeed no more than the artistic expression of these social, political, and religious institutions." [76] This applies, I might add, not just to architectural monuments but to every single element of the city.

The way we carry and dress ourselves, the gestalt, so to speak, of our personal appearance, is generally how others perceive us. The same is true for the city. Its energy, temperament, and general state of being, are articulated through its gestalt. We reveal our identity to ourselves and others, either consciously or unconsciously, through our city's gestalt. Thus, cities become the manifestation of our social, economic, and cultural understanding of ourselves.

The historic center of Bath, for instance, communicates constancy and respect for the past. At the same time, its gestalt can also be interpreted as a symbol of ossification and hopelessness. The thirty-meter-high entrance to "The World's Largest Home Furnishings Showplace" in High Point, near Winston-Salem, North Carolina, was a naked appeal to consumer emotion. Built in 1985, it created an exhibitionistic display in the city's configuration. Since then, the building has become an absurd curiosity. And finally, Karl Marx Allee in East Berlin, built at the end of the 1960s, was an urbane image of social justice in the German Democratic Republic but subsequently turned into a Potemkin village.

Old town of Bath, Great Britain

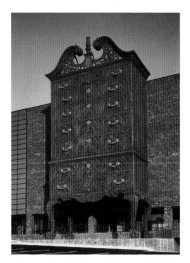

"The World's Largest Home Furnishings Showplace," Winston-Salem, North Carolina

Karl Marx Allee, Berlin

As I researched this book, I was constantly reminded how fragile and endangered our symbolic imagery truly is. Depending on the sensibility – individual or collective – continuity can rapidly become rigidity, and vitality quickly mutate into menace and disorder. This underscores the extremely fragile attitude we adopt toward our values and how the criteria that determine these attitudes are always subject to change, whether individual or collective.

Therefore there will never be a timeless or homogeneous gestalt of the city. Its momentary gestalt is a reflection of the patchwork of values held by its current inhabitants and builders, and by their predecessors. These all become layered on top of one another as the gestalt changes over time, following the watercourse way.

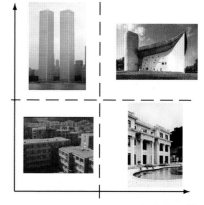

The qualitative dimensions of gestalt

THE AESTHETICS OF CITY GESTALT

Along with symbolic quality, aesthetics form the second dimension of complexity in a city's gestalt. The focus here is not on the meaning of the message but on its legibility. It concerns the intelligence or differentiation of the gestalt. Aesthetic power lies in the intensity with which symbols are made legible. Gestalt should reveal more than commonplace utility. In a building, load-bearing, supporting, and protecting have to be transformed into aesthetic gestalt. In an urban space, its functionality has to be interpreted through gestalt. It is not just a question of form, but also of structure. When form and structure are treated in a trivial manner, gestalt becomes illegible. When design is formulated with intensity, the gestalt becomes clear and distinct.

Philosopher Wolfgang Welsch's definition of aesthetics as the architect's opportunity to promote "a critical relationship with reality based in perception," as mentioned earlier in a quote by Marc Angélil, applies well in this context. Welsch writes that the opposite of

aesthetics is anesthetics, or in medical parlance, anesthesia, the state of no longer feeling or sensing. [77] In this state, the meaning of a city's symbolism is no longer understood and is replaced with a dull sense of staleness. In exploring the etymology of the word aesthetic, Welsch writes that it is derived from the Greek *aisthesis*, which means sensation or perception, feeling or revelation. The challenge of a city's aesthetics, then, is to find a gestalt that rises above vague forms and individual buildings and saturates the whole with meaning, thereby awakening our senses and challenging our perceptions. Dullness and coarseness weaken the intensity of our perception of the city.

Greatly simplified, the four-square diagram above illustrates this approach. On the bottom left, we find dull and irrelevant gestalt. On the bottom right, we find relevant yet dull gestalt. On the top left, we find clear yet dull gestalt. On the top right, we find intense and relevant gestalt that poignantly reveals societal values.

SYMBOLIC MEANING AND AESTHETICS IN CITIES

LINKING SPIRITUALITY AND GESTALT IN THE ANCIENT CHINESE CITY

Taoist culture draws on symbolic and aesthetic qualities. Taoist art and culture, while continuously seeking meaning in all things, are also characterized by a search for a refined aesthetic. We encounter signs of this effort in traditional Chinese script and art, as well as in its efforts to create and promote high-quality architecture and urban design.

Newly erected city gates reflecting the destroyed historic gates, Kunming, 2000

Linking Heaven and Earth with a Magical Line

The unity of heaven and earth, of nature and man, is one of the central tenets of Taoist philosophy. This theme must therefore also be incorporated into the gestalt of their cities. This connection is revealed through the use of virtual, and sometimes visible, lines that lead from a heavenly spot, usually a mountain or hilltop, to the city. [78]

Magic line connecting heaven and earth

Linking Heaven and Earth with Square and Circle

In the Imperial Palace of Beijing's Hall of Classics, built in 1906, the square represents the earth, the circle represents heaven. The house with the square base and the round peak combines the two. This symbol has archetypal power and to this day defines the gestalt of many important public buildings. In the seventeenth century, Michelangelo completed the rectangular basilica of St. Peter's with a dome. In the nineteenth century, the Capitol building was erected in Washington as a sequence of rectangles and circles. And at the end of the twentieth century, the German government insisted that the old rectangular Reichstag building be once more crowned with a cupola.

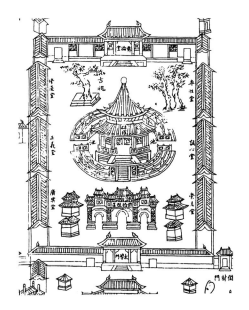

Square and circle connecting heaven and earth: The Hall of Classics in the Imperial Palace of Beijing, 1906

Outside the Square and Within the Circle

The design for The Hall of Classics integrates a game of circles and squares with the concept of the magic square with nine fields. Unnatural order, *Li*, is only applicable within the confines of four walls or enclosures. This unnatural order consists of social norms and ceremonial rites, invented by people to guide behavior and emotions, and to reflect these in architectural and urban form. Confucius, the Master of *Li*, declared at one time that everything "outside of the square," *fang wai*, did not concern him. [79]

The alternation between square and circle in the gestalt of houses depicts various degrees of worldliness where human intelligence and the force of nature alternate as the leading elements. Upon entering a Chinese garden – usually through a round gate – one is met by irregular shapes and curving motion. While the palace courtyard features only stones, the garden is dominated by water and plants.

The Sacred Field or the Magic Square

The carapace of the tortoise was used as a medium to convey messages from beyond the world of "the ten thousand things": it was laid into the fire, where it cracked, and the resulting lines were read as an oracle.

The *Luo-Shu* diagram is founded in this ritual. Like the carapace of the tortoise, it shows a square divided into nine fields. This magic square is a symbol for a fundamental order of the world that went beyond human comprehension. It became the symbolic plan for the Chinese city early on.

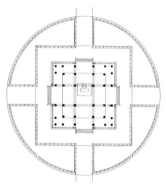

Layout for the Hall of Classics

The emperor of China consulting the turtle oracle, drawing from 1906

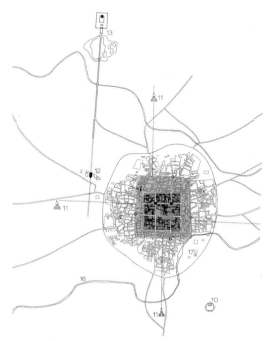

The Luo-Shu diagram, created in response to a command from heaven

TRANSFORMING THE GESTALT OF EUROPEAN RESIDENCES

Over time, our continuously changing values are reflected in how we choose to transform residential housing.

Two schools based on two different philosophical positions:

The medieval three- to four-story single-family home...

...evolves into the nineteenth-century multi-family home with social diversity from the *bel étage* to the attic.

After World War I, row housing represents the social revolution where *égalité* is now expressed in the gestalt of the city.

The growing belief in unlimited growth leads to yet another new type of residential building. The high-rise becomes the symbol of the 1960s.

With the post-World War II economic boom as well as the new mobility and affordability of automobiles, the detached single-family home becomes a new dominant building type.

In the beyond-the-modern era, old building types have lost their dominant force. They become patterns for solutions tailored to the needs of the site and the task.

Above all else, housing tends to mirror the state of mind of the individual. Public buildings, on the other hand, are powerful reflections of collective consciousness. This is especially true in the gestalt of school buildings. The following two contemporary school buildings tell stories of two entirely different worlds.

The first school, writes journalist Michael Egloff, "tactfully integrates a cool, modernistic architecture in the given situation. The building is monumental and powerful, and at the same time extraordinarily elegant, a contemporary school palace." [80] In the second school, writes its architect, Werner Seyfert, "The first and second grade classrooms are still characterized by a very protective and sheltering room plan ... In the third and fourth grade ... there is more emphasis on the front of the room, the teacher and the blackboard ... Whereas the room area where the pupils sit is still characterized by a free sense of openness in the sixth grade, it is fully concentrated in the direction of the teacher in the seventh grade ... For the tenth, eleventh and twelfth grade there is a fundamental shift in form ... The teacher is increasingly accepted as first among equals up to the point where the pupils join the teacher in a forum." [81]

When I returned from Egypt in 1961, I found a position in Jan Both's architectural office. He had been commissioned to design the Swiss Army pavilion at the Expo 1964 in Lausanne. My design for a studded dog collar as an archetypal symbol of national defense became the basis for the project. Celebrated artist Max Bill, apostle of modern art and famous for his abstract paintings, built the Swiss Art pavilion next door and was, understandably, horrified by my symbolic design.

The school building characterized by the belief in rationality...

Klasse 1   Klasse 5

Klasse 8   Klasse 12

...or the classroom layout in a Steiner school based on the evolution of consciousness in children

Swiss Army pavilion at the 1964 Expo in Lausanne, Switzerland, architect Jan Both

Signpost in Kyoto, Japan

—

AT THE VERY ROOTS OF CHINESE THINKING AND FEELING THERE
LIES THE PRINCIPLE OF POLARITY, WHICH IS NOT TO BE CONFUSED
WITH THE IDEAS OF OPPOSITION OR CONFLICT. IN THE METAPHORS
OF OTHER CULTURES, LIGHT IS AT WAR WITH DARKNESS, LIFE WITH
DEATH, GOOD WITH EVIL, AND THE POSITIVE WITH THE NEGATIVE,
AND THUS AN IDEALISM TO CULTIVATE THE FORMER AND BE RID
OF THE LATTER FLOURISHES THROUGHOUT MUCH OF THE WORLD.
TO THE TRADITIONAL WAY OF CHINESE THINKING, THIS IS AS INCOM-
PREHENSIBLE AS AN ELECTRIC CURRENT WITHOUT POSITIVE AND
NEGATIVE POLES, FOR POLARITY IS THE PRINCIPLE THAT + AND −,
NORTH AND SOUTH, ARE DIFFERENT ASPECTS OF ONE AND THE
SAME SYSTEM, AND THAT THE DISAPPEARANCE OF EITHER ONE OF
THEM WOULD BE THE DISAPPEARANCE OF THE SYSTEM.

___ *Alan Watts* [82]

YIN AND YANG

陰
陽

PREMISE
CARING FOR THE CONTINUOUS TRANS-
FORMATION OF CITIES MUST NEVER
BECOME A WAR OF TRUTHS, IDEOLOGIES,
OR DOGMAS. IT SHOULD BE UNDER-
TAKEN AS A GAME OF BALANCING LESS
WITH MORE, TOO LITTLE WITH TOO
MUCH.

One of the decisive transformations of the beyond-the-modern age is the dismantling of hallowed dogmas. We are in the midst of a spectacular deconstruction of the absolute truths that regulate economic order, church rule, political structure, and even the guidelines for urban design.

Modern consciousness waged a long and passionate battle against the structures and conventions of the pre-modernist era. Once the enslaving alliance between the church, politics, science, and art was finally broken apart, the battle gradually turned into all-out war in the twentieth century. Renewal was no longer anchored in a polarity between too much and too little, it had mutated into absolute truth. It no longer promoted the dignity of man, instead it reduced him to a foot soldier of an ideology. "Those who worship past and future, reactionary remembrance and utopian dreams, are the ones who instigate persecution and lead wars," [83] Aldous Huxley commented about late modernism.

Alan Watts, however, proposed a radically different world. The struggle for truth is a game of too much versus too little. The warring prophets must answer to a higher authority, one that weighs the different positions against each other and helps transform monologues into dialogues. In this way, change does not deteriorate into a linear process that leads to a supposedly ideal and perfect world; instead it becomes a response to new conditions, the conscious transformation of a position in space and time.

This fundamental difference between Eastern and Western attitudes is evident in the differing interpretations of the nature of the world. Aristotle declared that the world is divided into four distinct elements: earth, air, water, and fire. This concept formed the basis of Western natural sciences for centuries. Alchemy alone rejected this division and preserved the ancient unity. In the Taoist worldview, the elements are but fleeting conditions in a constant state of flux. Fire transforms wood into earth, earth produces metal, which in turn generates water, which nourishes wood. The *I Ching*, which contains the key teachings of Taoist wisdom, is therefore called the *Book of Changes*.

In a previous chapter I explained how urbanism – in contrast to science, art, and philosophy – was one of the last disciplines to integrate modernist principles. It was the technological developments of the nineteenth-century that eventually forced cities to join the modern age.

When Indian architect Mulkarj Anand asked Le Corbusier – then designing Chandigarh, the joint capital of India's Punjab and Haryana states – about the significance of local traditions, Le Corbusier reportedly replied: "What sense do local customs and habits make, once you say yes to the machine, to trousers and to democracy? [84] The concept of the machine as a metaphor for the cosmos dates back to the Renaissance; but it is only in the twentieth century that it became employed as a metaphor for the city.

In the beyond-the-modern age, the continued transformation of city is once more a game of balancing more with less, too much with too little. The game now has many dimensions: uniformity versus complexity, change versus continuity, artificiality versus nature, elitism versus social justice, economic dominance versus social dominance, and global uniformity versus localism.

The juxtaposition, at right, of the two paintings by Breughel reveals the multiple *yin* and *yang* aspects of the city. Both paintings illustrate the concept of polarity within the city. The energies of too much or too little transformation, the conflict between uniformity and complexity, and the dialogue between the local and the global, overlap and eventually merge together.

The uncontrolled and disrespectful craving for novelty and uniformity that characterized the Tower of Babel ultimately led to its collapse. It was impossible to find a common language. In the image of the Dutch village, there appears to be a complete lack of desire for renewal. Like a carousel ride, the same old stories get told over and over again. The city decays in its own smugness and does not allow new perspectives to develop. This once again brings to mind the aforementioned quote by Carl Jung: "For, just as completeness is always imperfect, so perfection is always incomplete."

Pieter Breughel, *Tower of Babel*, 1563

Pieter Breughel, *The Battle Between Carnival and Lent*, 1559

Getreidegasse in Salzburg, Austria   Eighth Avenue in Manhattan, New York

The four mythical creatures of China: the blue dragon, the white tiger, the red bird, and the black turtle with the snake. The top points south.

Yet cities also need the continuity provided, on a physical level, by technical infrastructure. Streets, sewers, and tram, train or subway lines define the structure of a city for generations to come. The same applies on a sensory or emotional level. People need continuity in the open spaces of the city in order to find their way and feel at home. This continuity is indispensable for the social, economic, and cultural quality of the city.

Determining whether an existing structure is more important than a new one, or whether something new is indeed necessary to preserve the vitality of the city, will always be an issue. It is also important to consider, however, whether newness is just a Utopian dream employed to destroy ingrained habits and beliefs, or, conversely, whether the forces resisting innovation are in fact driven by fear of change and inspired by reactionary memories. As Oscar Wilde challenged, it is "imperfection, not perfection, which needs our love." [85]

What applies to people also applies to cities. Efforts at achieving perfection and completion are doomed to fail when building cities is viewed as a finite production rather than a vital, never-ending process. In a more positive light, the quest for perfection can also be described as transformation in the interest of new needs, and the quest for completion as preservation of the continuity required by the life of the city.

In Taoist mythology, the confrontation between what exists and what is new, and between the complete and the perfect, is articulated through the ongoing struggle between the blue dragon and the white tiger. This is the rivalry between the masculine energy of the eastern morning and the feminine energy of the western evening. It remains the oldest and, to this day, the most relevant theme in caring for the transformation of the city.

People and cities need newness because their needs always change, and in the process, new goals and hopes arise. These needs, goals, and hopes are necessary for survival on the physical plane. They ground us in the feelings and sensibilities of the day and allow us to intuit the depths of the spiritual world.

Ever since I first began working in the field of urbanism – as an archaeologist in Egypt; an urban planner in Europe, Africa, and Asia; a civil servant and politician in Switzerland; and finally, as an expert on panels, at workshops, and in competitions throughout Europe – I recognized that the central theme of my work is dealing with polar energies. The themes are always different and yet similar. Transformation must be weighed against continuity, uniformity against complexity, globalism against local identity. Each project may have its own focus, but its roots are always planted among many polarities. I shall illustrate this with three examples.

YIN AND YANG IN OWERRI, NIGERIA

In 1976, when I asked Ogbonna Ukelonu, the Honorable Commissioner of Housing and Public Works for Imo State, one of Nigeria's newly created states, about the meaning of certain local traditions, I received the same answer as Mulkarj Anand had many years before from Le Corbusier. Only this time, the roles were reversed. I, the foreigner, was interested in preserving the local heritage while the local inhabitants were primarily interested in becoming a city of the world. "They will talk to you about African identity," Ukelonu told me. "Forget about it. Look at me. I wear an English suit and a French necktie. The fashion is the same all over the world. We want a town like Paris or London."

His government had hired me to plan the new city of Owerri, which was to be the capital of Nigeria's newly created southeastern Imo State. I ended up overseeing its construction for four years. Twelve thousand civil servants had to be relocated to Owerri as quickly as possible in order to run the new state. After the secession of the Ibo people from the centralized state had failed, the Nigerian government split the former East-Central province into two parts. The new southern province with its five million inhabitants needed a new capital. To the Ibo, this project had tremendous political significance. Having lost the war of secession, they wanted to proclaim their identity, competence, and creativity through this project. Three clans from old Owerri – a small market town with roughly thirty thousand inhabitants – had joined forces and offered seventy-three square kilometers of land for the development of the new city. Thus, the very place where the Ibo had mounted their last stand in the Biafran war, was selected.

On my first trip to Owerri, the only foreigners I ever came across were a small group of Americans. They had set up a radio antenna next to a large truck and took turns sitting

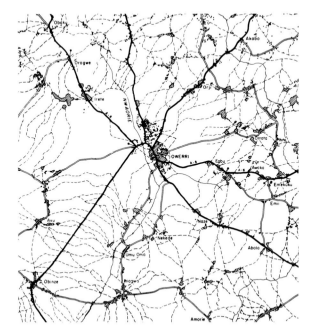

The market town of Owerri prior to the construction of the capital of Imo State

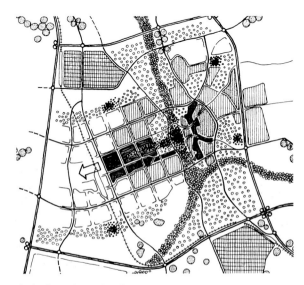

The development concept, 1976

118

Aerial shot of Owerri from the southeast

"The town planning consulting firm from Switzerland, Fingerhuth
and partners, which won the contract to prepare a master plan
for the development of Owerri as capital of Imo State (see photo above),
has submitted the final action report to the State Military Governor, Lt.
Commander Ndubuisi Kanu, at a short ceremony at the Government
House, Owerri." From the *Daily Star*, Owerri, December 10, 1976

Airplane wrecks from the Biafran war on the road to Owerri

Across from our camp where we kept our freight containers...

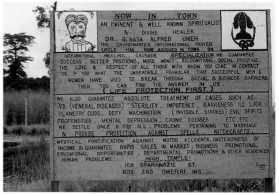

...the "Divine Healer Dr. G. Nasa Alfred Umeh" advertised his magic services.

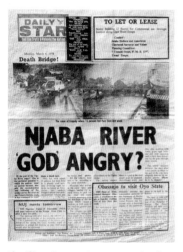

The *African Star* ran a story reporting that the Juju, the small tree spirits, were unhappy because they had not been honored when their trees were cut down to make way for the new road. This was why, the report claimed, trucks were crashing into the bed of the river.

I visited the young chief of a large family. At his side sat a man dressed as a woman. (S)he had also been the chief's predecessor's "representational wife." Since the wives of the former chief had always fought over the honor of sitting at his side, he had chosen his best friend to fill the role of wife instead. For simplicity's sake, his successor, whom I was visiting that day, decided to keep things just as they were.

inside with headphones to link Owerri to the world via satellite.

Twelve thousand civil servants, each with a family of five, and each creating the need for two more jobs – so, a total of two hundred thousand new inhabitants – clamored for housing in Owerri. And to what kind of town did they want to move, a town "like Paris or London," I wondered?

I tried to become involved in housing development, hoping to draw on my experience with assisted self-help where qualified craftsmen assist residents with technical aspects like electricity and water supply. I wondered whether the traditional form of collective property ownership for extended family could be maintained in some way. "This is not your business," I was informed.

Once the master plan for the new city had been approved, the government decided to create the Owerri Capital Development Authority (OCDA). This institution hired me to oversee the construction of the new city. In addition to streets, water supply, drainage, sewage, and street lighting, we also built the OCDA's administration building. We tried our very best to draw on local traditions. We planned just a single story, properly oriented to shield from sunlight, built with local timber, cross ventilation, broad cantilevered canopies, and a planted inner courtyard. Once construction was completed, I was called before the minister. Had I never seen a professional European journal, he inquired? This was not a ministry, he said with irritation, this was a shed.

And thus it continued. I had proposed building a stadium at the far end of the central row of public buildings, where an efficient regional public transportation system might one day be developed, and where noise emissions would not become a nuisance. When I presented my first draft of the plan to the governor, he asked somewhat sarcastically whether I had ever been to a soccer game.

Settlements financed by the World Bank

The Owerri Capital Development Authority's administration building

Peter Nwogu, the General Manager of OCDA, sitting in front of the master plan

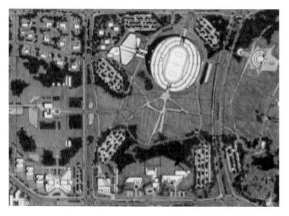

The search for the stadium site

The Minister of Sports of Imo State

Then he pointed to a different and very central site that just happened to be right next to his official residence. "You know, football is something very close to our hearts," he said. I asked if he really wanted all that noise right outside his bedroom window. He noted patiently that I clearly had no understanding of soccer. During a match, he would be sitting in the stadium, not at home.

Despite my obvious lack of soccer knowledge, the Minister of Sports nevertheless asked me to plan Owerri's stadium. He had been president of the Nigerian Olympic Committee for many years and was familiar with soccer stadiums around the world. Although I suggested he collaborate with Nigerian architects for the project, he repeatedly urged me to accept the job, despite my experiences with the governor. He knew exactly what he wanted and urged me to draw on my knowledge of the great European stadiums. He wanted an entrance like Berlin's Olympic stadium, a playing field like Lazio Roma, stands just like Stuttgart's *Neckarstadion*, and dressing rooms like London's Crystal Palace. I still declined the request. I did not want to build a European stadium in Nigeria.

We were constantly confronted with conflicts between old and new and between local and global elements. We felt, for instance, that it would be smarter to install roundabouts, a system that was gaining popularity throughout the world at that time, rather than electrically operated traffic signals. Among other reasons, we favored this solution because of Owerri's periodic power failures. The local vernacular for the Nigerian Electric Power Authority's acronym, N.E.P.A., was "Never Expect Power Always." We built the roundabouts but this solution failed to convince them. They believed that traffic must not be left to its own devices right in the middle of the city. So they stationed policemen at the intersections of the roundabouts. Due to the size of the roundabouts, however, a policeman had to be placed at each of the four merging lanes. After the grass on the central

One of Owerri's new roundabout intersections

circle grew so tall that the four policemen could no longer see each other, we abandoned this attempt at developing new global solutions.

I thus found myself in a difficult position. The polarity between global and local forces had become a trap for me. My decision to favor global sensibilities, such as sustainability and social commitment, were perceived as a new form of imperialism that undermined local progress. My attempts to integrate local elements failed as a result of the same problem. Neither corresponded with the visions of Imo State authorities. On the other hand, I could not identify with their version of the modern global language. They yearned for international significance and longed to abandon their local identity. The game of polarities simply failed to get underway.

Given this constant conflict, I resolved to engage primarily in those issues that dwelt outside of these polarities. I abandoned all attempts to initiate new housing policy and refused to plan the soccer stadium. I focused on completing the important things that needed to be done well. Primarily, I had to ensure the rapid development of the most robust, economical, and durable urban infrastructure possible. I gave up on art and philosophy and focused my efforts on science – in other words, the technical aspects of building a city. On this level, urbanism was quickly reduced to mere urban design. While this was no doubt useful in its own way, it certainly did not exhaust the project's full potential. Perhaps I was simply too young to take advantage of this opportunity.

A network of roads had to be built...

...to provide access to development plots.

YIN AND YANG IN BASEL, SWITZERLAND

After being elected city architect of Basel in 1979, I was once again confronted with technical and functional duties. My job was to maintain existing public facilities and to respond to new public needs by constructing functional and inexpensive buildings. I could have concentrated solely on these responsibilities but I couldn't ignore the fact that a completely different assignment needed my attention. A more than twenty-year-old war was being waged right in the center of town. There were two distinct factions.

One was still deeply rooted in classic modernism and fighting to preserve the values of a waning era. Much like Descartes' viewpoint mentioned earlier, they were convinced that "those ancient cities that were once mere villages and in the course of time have become large towns are usually so poorly laid out, compared to those well-ordered places that an engineer traces out on a vacant plain as it suits his fancy." The existing city had become an annoyance to its inhabitants. Following Cartesian principles, a comprehensive plan for redeveloping Basel had been approved in the 1960s. But this grand vision for a bright modern city ultimately collapsed. Plans for a four-lane highway right through the center of town, and for demolishing large portions of the old town, were scrapped. Nevertheless, veterans from the modernist army and their ideologues remained camped out in Basel. They were still dedicated Cartesians.

Basel extends into three countries: Germany, France, and Switzerland.

Three bridges and three ferries link Greater Basel and Lesser Basel.

Their opponents in this war were the preservationists whose emotions and sensibilities had been profoundly wounded in this ideological war. As far as they were concerned, the city was complete and any further changes would be a loss. Safeguarding the continuity of the city was, in their view, the primary task of urbanism

In my role as city architect, I had to avoid becoming the general of either of these battling factions. But I did have to face the conflict. I tried to transform the war into a game, one that could be played out on the level of the city's gestalt, its structure, form, and symbols.

The medieval market square with the town hall in the center of Greater Basel

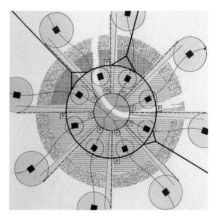

Comprehensive plan by the professional associations for the transformation of the city of Basel, 1963

Only 600 meters of the planned 10-km-long four-lane highway around the center of town were built. For decades, this stretch separated the train station from the heart of the city's downtown section.

IMBERGÄSSLEIN

The Imbergässlein is a romantic steep alleyway, just a few meters wide, which runs from
the marketplace up to the western plateau
of Basel. This is the densest section of the old
town. The houses are narrow and tall; there
is little light and hardly any sunshine. In the
1940s, the Cartesians slated it for demolition.
Inspired by plans for running a new, broad
street through the old section of town,
an urban renewal project was developed and
approved for the demolition of the historical
town center. A large square was to be created
at the center of the network of historic alleys
to clear space in the old market square for
motorized traffic. Structures from the Middles
Ages, with elements dating back as far as the
tenth and eleventh centuries, were earmarked
for demolition and the lane in question – the
Imbergässlein – was to be swallowed up by
the market square.

In the 1970s, the great period of the blue
dragon began to draw to a close.
A short stretch of the road was built, but
construction came an abrupt end when the
building lines for the valley bypass were
annulled. A gradual power takeover by the
antimodernists began to unfold.

In the first phase, a basic consensus was
reached that only historic exteriors and
facades should be preserved. New buildings
were to be erected behind these facades.
The necessary financing was approved by
parliament, but the antimodernists resorted
to a referendum and the proposal received
such a slim majority that a recount was
ordered. Years went by as appeals and counter-
appeals were filed back and forth. When the
legal situation was finally resolved, the fronts
had shifted so drastically that the renewal
projects had to be sent back to the drawing
board.

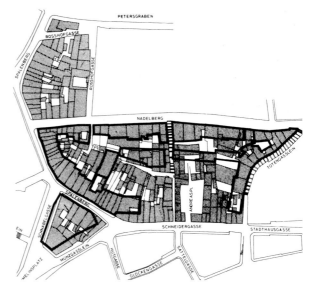

Project for the urban renewal of Basel's old town in 1949.
The buildings that are not blocked out in black were to be demolished.

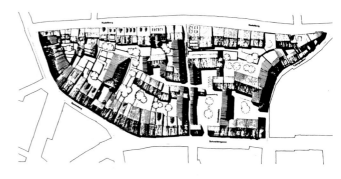

In 1970, the heart of the old town was still slated for demolition.
Now, however, the plan was to rebuild from within, leaving
the streetside historic facades intact.

Three multi-story houses were to be converted into twelve small apartments with one central stairwell.

In 1978, a project was developed that respected the historic fire walls and roof structures. The three houses were still to be converted into a three-story multifamily dwelling.

In the second phase, the fundamental structure of the historic buildings was taken more seriously. Fire walls and roof structures had to be preserved, but the internal structure of the houses was still subjected to radical changes. Houses 27 through 31 along the Imbergässlein, for instance, were combined functionally into a single structure by means of a central stairwell and three horizontally connected apartments. I joined the process in its third phase. The buildings still existed in their original state, I ensured that renovations preserved this condition.

It soon became essential, I realized, to institutionalize a new game for the gestalt of the city that involved the play between continuity and change, tradition and innovation, new and old, at other locations. A game anchored in the energies of this emerging time.

In the final stage, the three buildings were renovated as four-story single-family homes, just as they had been originally conceived in the Middle Ages.

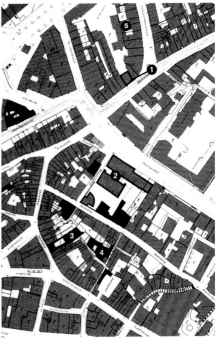

1 Spalenvorstadt 11, 2 Rosshof, 3 Spalenhof, 4 Imbergässlein 27-31, 5 Schützenmattrasse 13

ROSSHOF

Around the same time, a large lot in the old town presented an opportunity for staging the first move in this new game of the city. A spacious garden, nestled between the houses along the Nadelberg alleyway and the twelfth-century city wall, had remained undeveloped for eight hundred years. It belonged to a sizeable mansion which, although it looked like an eighteenth-century-style home, was in fact constructed in several layers in the manner of a Russian doll. Through a two-phase competition, we sought a gestalt suitable for a beyond-the-modern structure. We wanted a concept that respected the history of the place and at the same time clearly established a gestalt for our time. We sought to incorporate high-quality new public spaces into the old town grid and intelligently integrate working and living spaces.

The old Rosshof with its garden between Nadelberg and Petersgraben

After World War II, the garden was used as parking space for visitors to the old town.

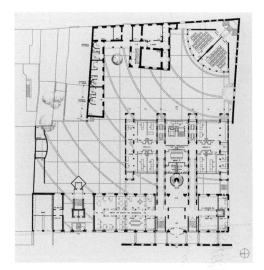

Zurich firm Naef Studer + Studer won the competition for the Rosshof development. The massive walls in the interior of the old Rosshof are part of a residential tower from the ninth century.

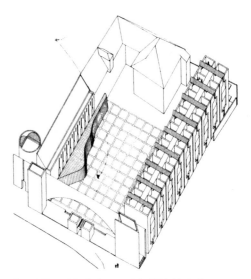

Competition entries that were not short-listed, including a very confident project by Mario Botta...

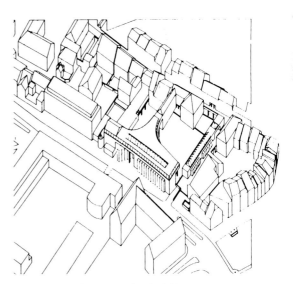

...an elegant project by Beatrice and Michael Alder...

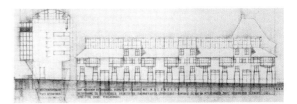

...and Herzog & de Meuron's proposal, for whose language the time wasn't yet right

Reinterpretation of the historic city wall

Dialogue with the surrounding structures

I commissioned Basel artist Hannes Vogel to create the visual design for the interior courtyard of the Rosshof. The result was an engaging interaction between horse names (the word Ross in Rosshof is German for horse) and elements for the area's archeological excavations.

SCHÜTZENMATTSTRASSE

Competitions for building gaps were important experiences that allowed for experimentation with transformation and continuity.
I have already introduced two such examples,
the Hebelstrasse and Spalenvorstadt projects.
In the midst of a very heterogeneous setting,
the third example created an intense symbol
of the consciousness of our time.

Herzog & de Meuron won the competition
to fill the Schützenmattstrasse building gap.
Their layout and façade was unprecedented.
I know of no other building that combines
autonomous gestalt and respect for the continuity of the urban site quite like this one.

The building gap in the configuration of the city

View from the interior onto the cast-iron facade

LUZERNERRING

The principles of *yin* and *yang* should also be applied to the development of new neighborhoods. Uniformity versus complexity became the dominant theme during the planning stage for the new Luzernerring neighborhood.

City property for the development of three hundred apartments had become available on the edge of town. To the north, there were private gardens and the French border; to the west, the street was edged with housing development from the turn of the last century; to the south, there were narrow lanes with two-storied row houses from the 1930s; to the east, there was green space scattered with free-standing buildings from the 1950s and 1960s. My architectural colleagues advocated creating one competition for the entire site. But I was concerned that within this chaotic urban landscape, yet another autonomous and disjointed typology would emerge. I wanted to use this opportunity to underscore the heterogeneous quality of the individual parts of the neighborhood and make it acceptable as an urban reality. I also wished to harmonize the disparate parts and allow for a variety of architectural interpretations within the new development.

After forming a work group consisting of architects Urs Burkart, Bernhard Hoesli, Peter Berger, Hans Zwimpfer, and myself, we developed a coherent urban concept linking the different patterns. We established a sequence of public spaces, building heights, and access roads. This enabled us to define five building areas, seek developers for each part, and then organize separate architectural competitions for each area.

The Luzernerring area within the configuration of the city

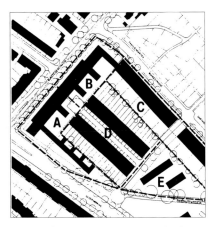

The urban planning concept as competition brief

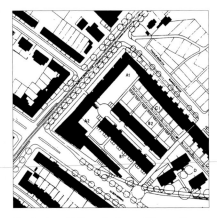

The site plan with the realized competition results

An entirely new neighborhood grew out of this process, one characterized by an integrated and concise urban plan and defined through clear language. At the same time, each of the five architectural components employed its own dialect, resulting in a highly differentiated and varied spatial arrangement within the framework of the greater order.

The new urban boundary to the north, designed by architect Michael Alder

The residential street in the interior of the neighbourhood. Ernst Spycher designed the development in the foreground and Vischer & Oplatek created the development in the rear.

Building along the Luzernerring, designed by architect Silvia Gmür as noise protection to the south

YIN AND YANG IN KUNMING, CHINA

By 1992, I had been city architect for fourteen years. Much like a bishop is responsible for his diocese, or a football coach for his team, my primary responsibility was to care for the city of Basel. Like Washington DC, Hong Kong, and Hamburg, Basel is a city-state. This means that the state tasks are not divided between the city and the canton. Part of my job description was to spend vast amounts of money each year on the transformation of the city. I oversaw many employees and, because my budget was so large, appeared to have many friends. Upon turning 56, the time seemed right to relinquish the authority that came with filling this public position. I felt ready to step down from wielding power in the external world, and wanted instead to gather experiences from other realms in order to, among other things, write this book.

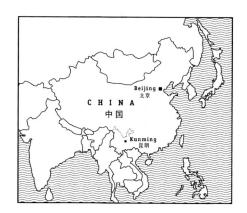

China with Kunming as the capital of the Yunnan province

If one attentively interprets the signs of the time, new opportunities frequently present themselves. Soon after resigning as Basel's city architect, I received a call from an old friend. Engineer Ernst Joos was the project manager for the city partnership between Zurich and China's Kunming. He inquired whether I would be interested in getting involved in the partnership's urbanism projects. In the first stage of the collaboration, the city of Zurich had provided support for Kunming by solving problems related to water supply and sewage removal. The next phase would address public transportation. My task would be to integrate public transportation into the urban configuration.

View from the old city toward the outside...

Public space within the old city...

...and toward the inside

...and public space within the new city

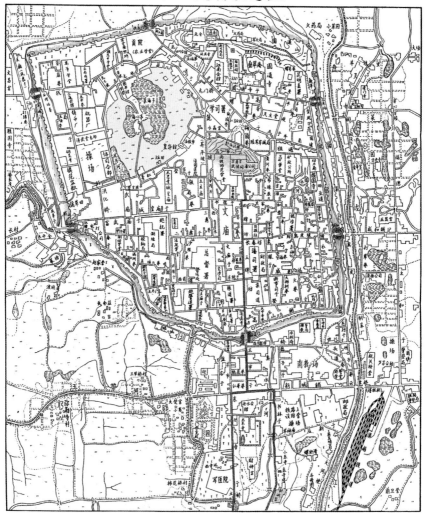

清末昆明街道图

The urban plan for Kunming in 1909. The new train
station for the narrow-gauge railway to Hanoi, which is still
in operation today, is visible on the bottom right.

136

Today, Kunming is the capital of the Chinese province of Yunnan, which lies north of Vietnam and east of Myanmar (formerly Burma). The city was reportedly founded in the eighth century as a fortification against the armies of the Tang dynasty. At that time, its walls bordered the shores of Lake Dian. Today, the lakeshore has retreated five kilometers south of the historical city. Around 1000 AD, during the reign of the Dali Kingdom, the city was expanded and flood ramparts were added. When the Mongolian crown prince Kublai Khan conquered the Dali Kingdom in 1254, a new city was erected on top of the ruins of the old city. When the first emperor of the Ming dynasty reorganized the imperial administration, the city was once again reconstructed. [86] Kunming was first connected to the West at the end of the nineteenth century when a railroad line was built linking it to Hanoi, which was then part of the French colony of Indochina.

In his travel diary, Marco Polo writes about Kunming: "At the end of the five days [the traveller] reaches the capital of the kingdom, which is called Yachi, a large and splendid city. Here there are traders and craftsmen in plenty. The inhabitants are of several sorts: there are some who worship Mahomet, some idolaters, and a few Nestorian Christians ... There is a lake there, some 100 miles in circumference, in which there is a vast quantity of fish, the best in the world. The natives eat flesh raw – poultry, mutton, beef, and buffalo meat. The poorer sort go to the shambles and take the raw liver as soon as it is drawn from the beasts; then they chop it small, put it in garlic sauce and eat it there and then." [87]

By 1990, large areas of this "magnificent imperial capital" still existed in the older sections of the city. In the central area around the bird market, the medieval town structure as well as many rows of historic houses remained in place.

In Owerri, I had been asked to create a new city. In Basel, my job was to care for the city's transformation. On my journey to Kunming, I had neither a mission nor formal responsibilities; but I had packed Alan Watts' *Tao: The Watercourse Way* in my suitcase. Up to that point, the two partner cities had focused on the transfer of technical knowledge. The experts from Zurich offered suggestions for expanding the water supply and improving the sewage treatment plants. They organized a traffic count as the basis for the construction of a network of tramlines and designed a system for more efficient intersections. My very first request was to be allowed to listen to what our partners in Kunming had to say. It turned out that, rather than worrying about how to optimize public transportation, they were preoccupied with entirely different concerns. They were caught up in the midst of an epic *yin/yang* conflict. During my first exploration of Kunming, all conversations circled around a single subject: the construction, within a few weeks' time, of a new central thoroughfare straight through the historic city. There was still no decision about what should be done with the remaining old city.

For sixty-year-old Chen Xinghua, the director of Kunming's city planning office, it was clear that the remaining historic inner city had to be demolished. "Wood is not a lasting building material," he announced, although the buildings in the old town had been built centuries ago. He believed in the new world of global modernism. When discussions turned to possible uses for street space, his advice was to "kill the bicycles," in order to make way for the growing flood of cars. The world had become a difficult place for Wang, the director's approximately forty-five-year-old deputy. On the one hand there was the traditional loyalty to *Lao*, the old, and on the other hand Wang was searching for more differentiated solutions without being allowed to express them. And then there were the thirty-year-old project leaders like Miss Gao, who appeared interested in preserving the old city but unable to assert themselves. They tried to preserve the image of Old Kunming by proposing new buildings that were

Renming Road, autumn 1996

Renming Road, spring 1997

Renming Road, autumn 1997

Renming Road, spring 1998

designed to look artificially old and would be erected over underground parking garages.

When there is a cultural conflict like that, one cannot enter the scene as an expert. I remembered Needham's remark that the Chinese had never sent missionaries to other countries. To avoid being considered a missionary, I had proposed that my participation be only in the form of dialogue. I assembled a team of friends whom I knew to be highly capable at both design and dialogue. The group included architects Karin von Wietersheim, Lisa and Matthias Wehrlin, and Zhao Chen. We organized a series of workshops with the administration of Kunming in which we all identified problems, created and evaluated solutions, and then presented proposals to the relevant political authorities. This set a fascinating political process in motion that lasted more than four years. We frequently met with our friends in Kunming and were confronted with new challenges each time. On each new visit we also had the opportunity to explore old challenges in more depth.

Workshop at the Kunming Urban Planning and Design Institute

We arranged with Chen Xinghua that we would work with his people for two weeks at a time in a room at the city planning office. Each session's theme was agreed upon during the previous trip and each workshop opened with a very formal session attended by the deputy mayor and his department heads. At the end of each workshop, we presented a set of plans we had developed and a preliminary report in English and Chinese. These plans formed the basis for our final reports and later only required polishing and editing.

The first workshop in 1996 dealt with how to care for the historic city. I tried shifting the conflict from a formal technical level to a cultural one. I felt strongly that the convictions for or against the old city and the corresponding urban strategy had to be rooted in the politics and administration of the city. To help the process along, we used sketches of alter-

The pharmacy

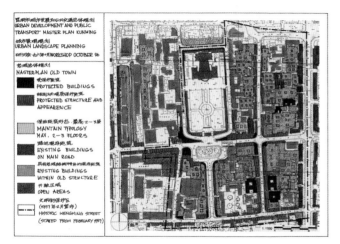

Inventory of the existing buildings

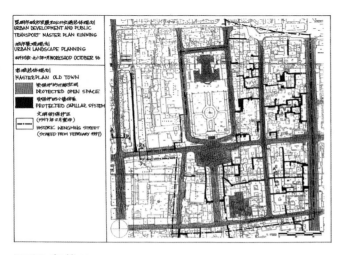

Inventory of public space

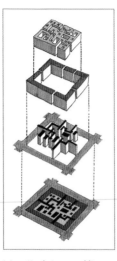

Interaction between public space
and development

native strategies showing the different polarities between innovation and continuity, globalism and localism. At the same time, it was important to present methods for implementing the alternative strategies.

By the end of the workshops, the city's planning office representatives pleaded to preserve the old city, a position their bosses then also favored and eventually acted upon. In subsequent workshops, we explored several aspects in more depth. Using one block of buildings in the old town as an example, the various typologies of traditional houses were documented and their potential for other uses demonstrated. Experts in monument preservation from Zurich organized courses for employees of Kunming's building authority teaching inventory methods for historic buildings. With the help of Zhao Chen, now a professor for architecture at the Nanjing University, but at that time our irreplaceable linguistic and cultural translator, a detailed inventory was taken of one of Kunming's most beautiful courtyard houses. The owner later received our technical support during the renovation. Since then, the house was given the UNESCO Asia-Pacific Heritage Award.

I discuss this with such detail because I am convinced that an awareness of the importance of this type of collaboration is crucial in the context of caring for the transformation of cities. Linking the various levels of detail, approaching each task with an interdisciplinary manner, and encouraging close collaboration among all of the city's partners, are crucial elements for successfully transforming a city. The success of our work was underscored by the Kunming municipal council's decision to ban any future changes to the old town center around the bird market.

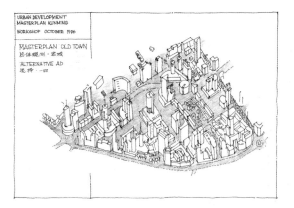

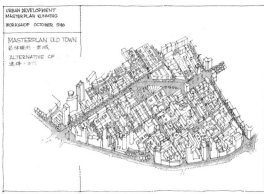

The first alternative concept, specifically featuring the polar positions of transformation and globalization

The second alternative concept, specifically featuring the polar positions of continuity and localism

原则性的实施
LEGAL IMPLEMENTATION

文明街传统风貌保护区规划
昆明规划院 1998 年 10 月制订
ORIGINAL PROTECTION PLAN OF KUPTI
FOR THE TRADITIONAL DISTRICT OF
WENMING STREET, 10.1998

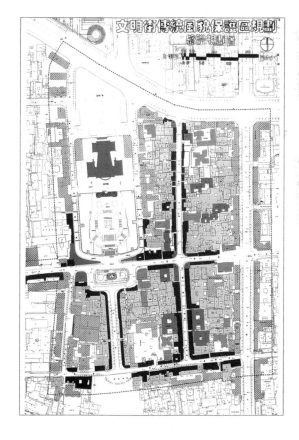

完全保护建筑
PROTECTED BUILDINGS

结构和外观受保护建筑
PROTECTION ZONE
structure and appearance

保留建筑形态
CARE ZONE FOR NEW BUILDINGS
scale and typlogy

须与传统街区风貌 协调的建筑
BUILDINGS
to be coordinated with traditional buildings
and urban structure

建议撤迁建筑
PROPOSAL TO BE REPLACED

传统风貌街区保护界线
LIMIT OF PROTECTED AREA

昆明市规划院一九九八年·风上提方案
KUPTI 1998.10 Protection Plan

Plan approved by the governing council of the city of Kunming
in 1997 for the preservation of the old town of Kunming

Drawing, lithograph by M.C. Escher, 1948

—

TAO DOES NOTHING AND YET NOTHING IS LEFT UNDONE.

— *Lao-tzu* [88]

無爲

08 WU WEI

PREMISE:
THE CENTRAL TASK OF THE URBANIST
IS TO OVERSEE THE GAME MINDFULLY
AND WITHOUT PREJUDICE.

The Chinese ideogram for *wei* is derived from the image of an elephant with a human hand holding its trunk. *Wei* symbolizes comprehension and dexterity, but also making, doing, acting, and controlling. *Wu* stands for negation or denial. Thus, *wu wei* is the denial of *wu*. Watts writes that the person living in Tao understands the wisdom of acting without violence and follows the 'Watercourse Way,' because everything in life is in flux. [89] As described by John Blofeld in *Taoism: The Quest for Immortality*, "*Wu wei*, a cardinal principle of Taoists, literally means 'no action' ... it means avoiding action that is not spontaneous, acting fully and skillfully by all means but only in accordance with present need." [90]

Consciousness of the contradictions inherent in "the world of the ten thousand things" calls for a different kind of thinking, sensing, and feeling. In the chapter about *yin yang*, I addressed what has become known in popular culture as the "end of the great truths." Foucault spoke of great truths as "mégarécits," and called for a "vigilance vis-à-vis that which is assumed as a given." I wish to clarify that acting mindfully, and cultivating an attitude of non-action, is not a call for passivity, resignation, or *laissez-faire*. On the contrary, it is

based in acute awareness, dedicated commitment, and the readiness to act when necessary. Following is advice from three experts in the art of mindfulness.

In verse 60 of the *Tao Te Ching*, Lao-tzu writes: "Governing a large city is like frying small fish." [91]

Sir Patrick Abercrombie, who designed the layout of greater London after World War II, offers similar advice. "A successful urban planner must have only three qualifications. He must be at least 40 years old. He must know that water only runs downhill. He must be able to listen." In this context, being forty years old and knowing that water only runs downhill means one must have experience in the world. By not getting caught up in things, one can achieve perspective and insight and thus avoid being swept up in polarized positions. Attentive listening allows for mindful action.

Philosopher Wolfgang Welsch employs comparable words. "Sensitivity is a fundamental requirement in a world of plurality. Attention to detail, mindfulness in relation to assumed givens, care for the nondescript, and flexibility and spontaneity, become important. A keen sense is necessary for determining differences between what appears identical. Moreover, one must be able to identify the core issue of respective complexes. Finally, one must find the fitting response to precarious situations full of conflict and disorder." [92]

The ability to listen, care, and be mindful are the key characteristics of another important aspect of beyond-the-modern urbanism; one that overcomes the modern urban planner's rational, linear stance, his monologue, and his obsessive fixation on the individual object.

"OUT OF CONTROL," OR FROM PUZZLES TO DOMINOES

Some time ago, my wife and I visited a street café in the old Moroccan port city of Essaouira. An English couple was seated beside us and began unwrapping a newly purchased game of dominoes. They asked us if we knew how to play. I had a vague idea and embellished my explanations with a remark concerning the importance of this game in regards to my profession. City architects and urban planners today, I said, no longer play with puzzles, only with dominoes. The Englishman seemed surprised by my comment. He then identified himself as Richard Rogers, the world-renowned architect known for having built, among many other projects, Paris' Centre Pompidou together with Renzo Piano.

So began a long conversation about the differences between puzzles and dominoes. A puzzle is a rigorously controlled strategic game with only one correct solution. The game is ruled by a specific image that has been broken into many fragments. The player's task is to reassemble the pieces until the image becomes visible. Only the sequence of assembling the pieces is undetermined and the player controls the progress of the game at every moment. The only existing order is that all the pieces must be assembled to match the image on the puzzle's box. The only variable is how long it will take to bring the whole puzzle into a state of order. No partner is required to assemble a puzzle, whereas at least two players are required to play dominoes. The strategy for playing dominoes, to use Welsch's words, is one of "finding the fitting response to precarious situations full of conflict and disorder."

In *Out of Control*, American biologist Kevin Kelly describes how a swarm of bees selects a new hive. In a cooperative process involving dozens of scouts, and without the queen bee's involvement, a consensus is reached with regard to the quality of various potential sites. The process is non-linear; it is based on the complex collaboration of many bees who, by expressing intense enthusiasm for a particular site, make selection possible. [93]

Certainly in terms of the evolution of our consciousness, we are far more advanced than bees. Still, I find this example fascinating. The quest for the ideal city and for control over urban development was one of modernism's most ambitious projects. The belief that complete control could be exerted over a city is a clear example of modern hubris. While we have succeeded in walking on the moon, cities still elude our control. I remember a visit to Tema, a new city in Ghana planned after World War II by the famous Greek urban planner Konstantinos Doxiadis. The site at which Doxiadis had planned to create the city center was now only occupied by an isolated bank and a hotel. Both buildings were surrounded by tall grass and a second-floor terrace – the meaningless remnants of what should have been a raised pedestrian passageway connecting a whole sequence of large buildings. The actual city center was now located far north, where the first Coca-Cola kiosk had been erected during the construction of the city.

In order to transform vulgar gestalt into aesthetic gestalt, cities require care and mindful attention combined with technical know-how and artistic ability. Far from showing respect toward the people for whom they are building, many architects still display a distinctly modern arrogance. I know that different laws often apply in the practice of architecture and that architects must also be warriors, capable of wielding a whip in order to parade their elephants through the city's arena. The architect must defend his own ideas as well as the interests of a client, prove his creativity as well as technical and

Place Moulay Hassan in Essaouira, Morocco

financial competence. But the drama and tragedy of the modern city is due to the absence of non-warriors. Taoist city architects and planners could transform warriors into players and battles into games.

In the urban circus, non-warriors should direct the performance. They should provide advice and support to the decision-makers for deciding which warrior should enter the ring at which time and for how long. In the urban soccer game, non-warriors represent the referees and they must blow a whistle when there is too much aggression or a lack of aesthetics. In the urban theatre, the non-warriors represent the audience and must show approval through clapping and disapproval through booing.

The issue in the beyond-the-modern age is one of too much versus too little, of a search for images that depict the way we want to be, of reintegrating that which has been excluded, and of implementing the new. We need people to look after the game of the city with care and attention. The power of the Taoist principle of *wu wei* would thus be revealed.

The city center of Tema, Ghana

I have chosen three examples from my professional practice for the purpose of illustration. In each instance, to use the descriptive words of philosopher Wolfgang Welsch, sensitivity, attention to detail, mindfulness, care, flexibility, and spontaneity come into play. The first example, the master plan for Basel's SBB train station, illustrates the background for the action; the second example, The Shit Architect, focuses on the need for mindfulness in action; and the third example, Downtown Winterthur, presents how attentive action can be organized.

MINDFULNESS AND SENSITIVITY

MASTER PLAN FOR BASEL'S SBB TRAIN STATION

The area surrounding Basel's Federal Swiss Railway station had become quite disordered in the 1980s. An ugly and uninviting section of urban highway, combined with the beginning and temporary stages of construction on an underground walkway accessing the train station, were all testimonies to failed visions for a new city. A bank tower and a large, box-like Hilton hotel remained as further autistic relics of the modern era. Large, deserted stretches of railroad land quietly rotted away to the left and the right of the station and on the far side of the tracks. For decades, the train station itself had been neither properly maintained nor upgraded to meet new needs.

At the same time, there was no shortage of needs, interests, and hopes for the site. The station, besides needing a more timely identity, also needed to expand with new tracks and platforms. The postal service needed a new distribution center. The city's tram operators wanted at least two tracks redirected so that passengers could reach the station without having to change trams. The area's economy needed attractive building lots for new businesses without having to displace residential neighborhoods and unleash vicious conflicts. Finally, the city's citizens were annoyed with the unpleasantness of the station's public space and wanted more attractive access to it.

In 1984, the government of Basel charged me with overseeing this project. Our goal was to develop a politically and economically viable urban concept within two years. In 1986, the governments of Basel's two adjacent cantons, the Swiss Federal Railway, and the Swiss Postal Service signed a letter of intent in which the four partners agreed to realize the project. Today, the essential elements have already been completed or are in the process of being completed.

Relics of modernism on Basel's central station square

The new station square, traffic-free and with an above-ground pedestrian link to downtown Basel

The new raised station overpass that replaced the underground passageway, designed by Spanish firm Cruz & Ortiz and Swiss firm Giraudi & Wettstein.

New tracks for the direct routes to the train station have been laid across the station square. Pedestrians access the station at street level without having to descend into in a subterranean labyrinth. The former underground passageway has been converted into a bicycle storage facility. The new station square is closed off to automobile traffic. A new attractive parking garage was constructed beneath the square. A new raised passageway provides access to the platforms and attractively links the large neighborhood on the opposite side of the station with the city. The fallow railway property is being reassigned to new, lucrative uses. Some of the buildings are completed, while others are still under construction. Numerous other newly-erected buildings in the neighborhood are providing a whole new face to the area. Because it radiates this new identity, the local economy is motivated to invest in the area. I estimate that nearly three billion Swiss francs have been invested in the project during the past ten years.

In Zurich, a similar project, where the planning costs reached ninety million Swiss francs, was abandoned after twenty years of planning. Why did we succeed in Basel? I would venture, perhaps over-enthusiastically and pretentiously, that our Taoist approach in the spirit of *wu wei* played an important role. We didn't grab the elephant by its trunk in order to pull it in a specific direction. Instead, we presented it with a vision that would become the goal of the journey. The path became the focus. It was the willingness to solve problems that was important, not how the problems were solved.

Still, problems were taken seriously. Instead of being interpreted as threatening interventions, however, they were dealt with as expressions of the unsolved aspects of our project.

We treated the collaborations and synergies between the individual endeavors with care and paid more attention to these than to partisan interests.

We tried to ensure optimal and continuous transparency concerning the project among all its participants and the public. Political concerns were given preference over technical concerns. And we tried to listen and to be mindful.

As the American sociologist Richard Sennet recently exhorted in Zurich, "We have to learn to talk to people."

The former freight depot area, designed by Basel architect Hans Zwimpfer, with the new tram lines for direct access from the suburbs to the train station, the first stage of office buildings, and the new postal distribution center

Construction of a Herzog & de Meuron-designed office building at the former French National Railways depot area

AN APPEAL TO CARING
AND FINDING THE FITTING
RESPONSE

"THE SHIT ARCHITECT," KARACHI

The city is a highly sensitive and complex
system with an extraordinary capacity to heal
itself. Urbanism is the therapy that promotes
this healing process. In order to be able to act
at the right place and the right time, respon-
siveness to the needs of the city is an indispensable prerequisite. Only mindfulness
and sensitivity, and a radical independence
from the familiar, will allow the urbanist
to discover where action is needed. The city
architect must possess strong intuition in
order to identify the level of action required
for a specific time and place.

I met Perween Rahman at a United Nations
conference about the city of the future and
the role of young architects. She was born in
Pakistan, had studied in Europe, worked with
renowned Dutch architect Rem Koolhaas,
and afterwards returned to Karachi. She introduced herself to me as "The Shit Architect."
She had devoted her mindfulness to Karachi's
sewers. She was convinced that working with
the water and sewage system was crucial in
the poorest neighborhoods of Karachi. Once
they become organized, communities are
able to maintain a fairly satisfactory standard
of housing and living. Yet a functioning
sewage disposal system is a basic prerequisite.
Unfortunately, this is one part of the system
which the local residents cannot influence
on their own. It must be managed within
a larger context. To this end, Rahman set up a
non-governmental organization (NGO) whose
mission it was to coordinate efforts between
the municipality, the local residential lobbyists, and the technicians in charge of the
construction and maintenance of the sewage
system. This interaction was an indispensable
prerequisite for establishing and maintain-
ing a minimum standard of living in the area.

Installation of water pipes by self-help organizations
in Karachi, Pakistan 94

As I experienced during my first job in a public
capacity, there are instances when urbanism
becomes very simple and where linear
and rational action is the only appropriate
approach. Hired to establish a regional planning office for the building department
of Switzerland's canton Wallis, home of the
Matterhorn mountain, I decided to start a
dialogue about goals and conflicts related to
the canton's regional development. We discussed conflicts between highways and nature
reserves, ski lifts and protected forests. We also
talked about which towns should be developed as regional centers and how this might
conflict with the autonomy of communities.
I rapidly became familiar with the cultural
conflict that existed between urbanism as a
political assignment to ensure the implementation of public interests, and this region's
deeply ingrained belief in the importance of

individual freedom. The most difficult planning task during these discussions was
establishing building development boundaries
to enable efficient sewage collection. Some-
how, the sewage project seemed to threaten
an ancient sense of personal freedom. There
is no need for such a project, claimed one
town's old council chair, because "once polluted water has run across a thousand stones,
it is clean again."

Then a typhoid epidemic broke out in the
resort town of Zermatt. It was suspected that
the disease had been caused by polluted
drinking water – likely the result of a leak in
the sewage system. People died. No one was
allowed to leave the valley. Suddenly urban
planning became crucial to the very survival
of people. The canton's government dispatched me to seek help from the director
of the Institute for Wastewater Management
at the Swiss Federal Institute of Technology.
I was now no longer engaged in negotiating
complex political conflicts and cultural para-
digms, but in the urgent technical need of
caring for the city. The city itself had drawn
attention to, and demanded, as Welsch wrote,
"the fitting response to precarious situations
full of conflict and disorder."

IDENTIFYING THE CORE
ISSUE AND FINDING
A FITTING RESPONSE

TRANSFORMING DOWNTOWN
WINTERTHUR

As already stated several times in this book
so far, I believe urbanism does not concern
the invention of the city but rather caring for
its transformation. We must find a way to effectively deal with matters that require action.
As Welsch writes, it is about "identifying
the core issue" and then "finding the fitting
response." Our traditional modern administrative hierarchies, institutional agencies, and
political systems are poorly equipped, and
sometimes even wholly incapable, of coping
with this different attitude toward action.
Beyond-the-modern urbanism calls for pro-
active behavior. The planning process for
the redevelopment of downtown Winterthur,
a former industrial city north of Zurich, provides a good example.

Winterthur's modern structure was laid out
in the second half of the nineteenth century.
It consisted of a network of tramlines, streets,
industrial parks, public buildings, and residential neighborhoods laid out around the
medieval center of the city. The traditional
tools, procedures, and institutions of modern
cities facilitated this transformation. Building lines, zoning plans, and construction laws
were used to determine what and where one
could, or could not, build. A departmentally
organized administration dealt with the various projects. The cityscape was dominated by
a tall high-rise building that was the administrative headquarters for Sulzer, an old
heavy-machinery manufacturer and the city's
largest employer. It appeared to have fallen
from the sky and landed in the very spot that
would best serve the company.

Winterthur's beyond-the-modern era began
in 1989. Radical changes in the world economy
threatened Sulzer's very existence. The company closed down large parts of its production facilities in Winterthur and tried selling

off the industrial real estate it no longer needed. To this end, and without prior consultation, Sulzer presented the municipal council with a development concept for building offices and housing on their old factory site.

The project reflected modernism's most negative characteristics. It was a conglomerate of cubes, a new autonomous urban neighborhood, entirely lacking any connection to its location. The existing city was considered irrelevant and treated with contempt. Open space was in fact leftover undeveloped space and given absolutely no consideration in the project. The project did not contain an autonomous and progressive identity; it did not do justice to its central position within the city, and it failed to interpret the area's character, which had evolved over time. The proposal was harshly criticized, especially since it was connected with the loss of several thousand jobs in the city.

This unfortunate situation led to a fifteen-year process during which I was invited to participate by developing tools, procedures, and institutions that would be relevant for a suitable transformation of the area in the beyond-the-modern age. From my perspective, developing downtown Winterthur – in keeping with all the principles of *wu wei* – exemplified a new approach to caring for the transformation of beyond-the-modern cities. There was no final plan. Instead, we developed a set of goals, a spatial vision, and rules of the game. These created the basis for a new urban concept.

The city's projects and urban concept were developed with intense public input, including an urban forum, two weekly workshops, and a multitude of competitions and expert reports. Each architectural project was deeply rooted in the urban concept as a whole.

Nothing new was invented; instead, existing elements were given context. By using as much care, respect, and innovation as possi-

Layout of Winterthur at the end of the nineteenth century

Train station and beginning of the old town (foreground), and the Sulzer industrial area (background)

ble, the situation's potentials were leveraged and an effort was made to develop a high-quality urban gestalt.

City authorities provided the internal organization necessary to ensure open inter-action between different levels of planning, to promote feedback, and secure the careful supervision of each individual project. Over a period of ten years, three external planning experts were engaged as consultants and a private-sector project leader was hired to oversee operations.

The project's successful flow was the result of a carefully maintained and ongoing dialogue between the city's various partners. From the public forums to the project evalua-tion juries, the dialogue was a give-and-take process, rather than a linear one. The prerequi-site for a successful experience was a political culture that viewed its city as an intricately connected economic, social, and cultural living space. Caring for beyond-the-modern cities is not about constructing the perfect city, or watching from a distance as a city runs its natural course. It is a dedicated process that involves caring for and working with the constantly emerging energies of the city; re-maining aware of its contradictions and com-plexity; always weighing too much against too little; continuously searching for aesthetic intensity; and repeatedly seeking grounding in social consciousness. Thus, it is the manner in which we engage in action or decision-making that becomes the most important element.

In modernism, the multidimensionality of the city was a threat that had to be overcome through rationality, order, transparency, and clarity. This required control. The law became the determining factor in social and political processes. Modernism thus developed and perfected legal tools, procedures, and institu-tions for caring for cities.

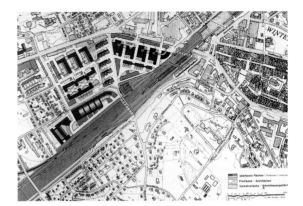
Project for new use, 1989

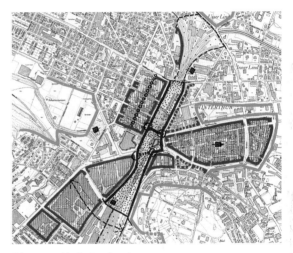
Urban concept for the town's center, 1992

Transformation of the Sulzer industrial area, 2004

Swisscom high-rise overlooking the train station, designed by
Urs Burkard, Adrian Meyer & Partners, Baden, Switzerland

instances where public interest must be respected on all counts.

The new tools, procedures, and institutions share the following common characteristics:
– They are non-linear and therefore operate in a cyclical and repetitive manner.
– They require networks that link the partners in the process.
– They are characterized by an awareness of the constant transformation of the city. This means that new ideas can be integrated at any time.
– They not only connect partners but also the various disciplines of the city.
– They ensure that the non-rational dimensions of the city are also taken into consideration.

Finally, when all is said and done, just as Lao-tzu wrote, governing a large city is like frying small fish.

The threat of multidimensionality is no longer relevant in beyond-the-modern consciousness. The time of simple guidelines, ultimate visions and plans, and hierarchical decision-making has passed. Our actions must be characterized by a new awareness of the complexity and contradictions of the world and its cities. The quest for quality within cities is no longer tied to implementing dogma; instead, it is a game with an endless variety of options and potential outcomes. We should define the rules of the game, develop strategies, and employ resources in an intelligent manner. Much like playing dominoes, we must play the game carefully, passionately, and beautifully. Once the game is in progress – and the game of the city is always in progress – the key is to be mindful, to seize the moment, and to develop synergies with each partner involved in the game of the city This requires new tools, procedures, and institutions. Founded in mindfulness, these are not set in stone and may take the form of visions, strategies, models, and regional development concepts. Laws and binding plans are secondary; they are especially important though in

Among the multitude of approaches, I would like to share three as examples illustrating the search for new paths: the urban concept as tool; the urban planning workshop as procedure; and the urban design advisory board as institution.

THE URBAN CONCEPT AS TOOL

The aim of urbanism is to interpret people's needs, goals, and dreams – crucial for a city's gestalt – in a manner that weaves social, economic, cultural, and aesthetic quality into the fabric of the city. Urbanism is the link between the city's various partners and disciplines and ensures continuity and transformation over time. The urban concept is the central tool that helps achieve this task: it establishes the structural order, the spatial potential, and the game rules for the city or parts thereof, and ensures that the expected level of quality is attained.

The urban concept mediates the relationship between spatial elements – lot parceling and development, open spaces and landscape, public buildings, traffic routes and infrastructure – and various levels of planning. In this manner, it provides a link between planning and architectural and technical projects. The urban concept evolves out of the interaction between different players – authorities, inhabitants, users, investors, property owners, and public-minded organizations – on the urban stage. One of the urban concept's essential tasks is to assess diverging interests. It is therefore usually managed and determined by public authorities and then binding for all levels of government. The urban concept functions as a declaration of intent and can therefore be authorized and changed by the executive at any time unless other provisions are made at the outset.

An urban concept may generally be designed to span ten to fifteen years. Should the concept's requirements, goals, and visions change fundamentally before that time, it can and should be adapted to the new conditions. Unless otherwise agreed, these changes are usually carried out following the same procedures used to develop the concept in the first place. The urban concept informs private partners about the public authorities' intentions. It is important that for each site and project, a specific urban concept be developed based on the site's content, characteristics, and required methods and procedures. These should be developed based on the specific characteristics and energies of each place and time.

In the following, the individual requirements of separate urban concepts are illustrated with examples from Owerri, Basel, and Kunming. They all serve the same purpose, yet their differing goals, contents, and evolutions clearly show the adaptability of the urban concept as tool. One of the planner's central tasks is to search for the necessary elements of the plan and the appropriate method to develop the concept. To effectively do so, this person needs creative design skills, an understanding of how cities function, the ability to listen and to understand each party's concerns, and plenty of patience and perseverance.

OWERRI

The urban concept for the center of Owerri
is an example of a standard plan to develop a
new piece of city. It contains and coordinates
streets and paths, building lots, open spaces,
and public buildings. Examples for possible
development are presented in the plan. They
indicate possible typologies for private buildings and locations for public ones. The concept also serves as a basis for infrastructure
development: water supply, wastewater
management, drainage, and power supply.

Parliament buildings of Imo State

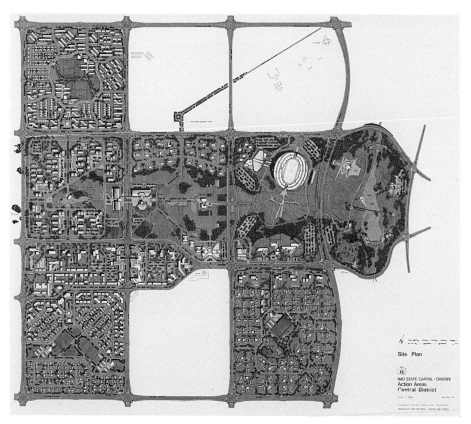

Urban concept for the center of Owerri with parliament,
Governor House, residences for the ministers and parliamen-
tarians, the ministry buildings, hotel and business center,
and three residential neighborhoods

Railway Station Area

To reconfigure an existing city neighborhood,
the urban concept must contain the proposed
measures through which the area is to be
redefined. The urban concept for the transformation of Basel's SBB train station area,
subsequently renamed Euroville, included as
its key elements:

– Integration of suburban tram lines (1)
– Redevelopment of the freight depot area
  into office buildings and construction of a
  new postal distribution center (2, 9)
– Expansion of railway yard with additional
  tracks (3)
– Conversion of the central station square (4)
– Construction of new raised pedestrian
  passageway across the rail yard (5) and
  new bypass around the Gundeldinger
  neighborhood (6)
– Construction of wider Münchensteiner
  Bridge (7)
– Development of the French National
  Railways area into office buildings (8)
– New shopping center combined with
  the new pedestrian passageway to
  the Gundeldinger neighborhood (10)

Gundeldinger Neighborhood

To preserve and convert an exising neighborhood, the urban concept must identify
the framework and strategy that will form
the basis for development and construction.
For instance, the urban concept for the
Gundeldinger neighborhood, directly adjacent
to Basel's SBB train station and developed
in conjunction with it, established guidelines
for fulfilling housing allotment requirements.
Other elements of the concept focused on
traffic, buildings that should not be demolished, and public space.

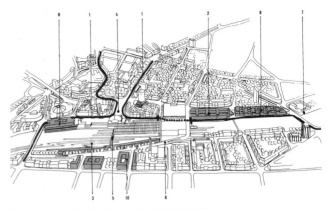

Urban concept for the Basel train station area master plan

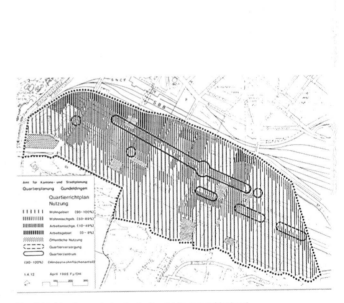

The district development plan for the Gundeldinger neighborhood
established guidelines for required levels of housing allotment.

St. Alban Valley

To transform an important historical neighborhood, there may sometimes be no need for a plan. The emphasis, in this instance, is on an attitude and strategy which all concerned parties must agree upon. The urban concept for the renewal of the Saint Alban Valley was developed without a plan. The investor, a non-profit organization called the Christoph Merian Foundation, and the city's administration, represented by myself as city architect, agreed on an approach that would form the basis for the area's renewal. Through a process of mutual consultation and agreement, new elements – public open spaces, a museum for contemporary art, a youth hostel, a paper museum, and a small cultural and crafts center – were gradually integrated into the historic structure.

St. Alban Valley around 1462

Urban concept for the renewal of St. Alban Valley

Apartment and commercial buildings on the upper Deichkopf, designed by Basel's Diener & Diener architectural firm

Kunming

Developing the vast area for the northern expansion of Kunming exemplifies another great challenge: how to combine large- and small-scale visions in order to eventually achieve the same goal.

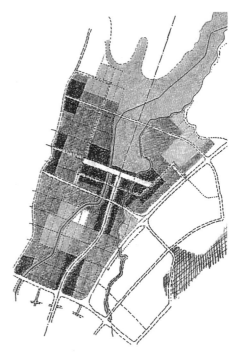

Urban concept for Kunming's northern city

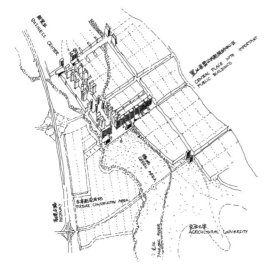

Urban concept for the center of northern Kunming, developed in collaboration with the Kunming Urban Planning and Design Institute, architect Matthias Wehrlin, and myself

Elaboration on the concept for the city's center

Model of the concept

THE WORKSHOP AS COOP-
ERATIVE PROCESS

Beyond-the-modern urbanism cannot be determined by an architect or engineer's isolated
vision, an artist's emotional design, or a
civil servant's lonely decision. In the Taoist
approach, the path is the essential component
of the completed vision for a place. In this
context, path signifies the shared journey of
each involved party. But there are no universal
guidelines for this path. Each project has its
own path and may range from a largely par-
ticipative process – which ensures grounding
but may prevent distinctive decisions – to
a highly elitist process. Each of the aforementioned examples followed its own path.
The following examples document these
distinctly different processes.

When redeveloping Basel's train station area,
I had to reach as many interested parties as
possible through a process as broad and open
as possible. By inviting these parties to collaborate as partners from the beginning, we
secured their commitment to the project
in the subsequent stages. This was important
because we had to win several public referen-
dums over the course of the project. Basel's
political decision-making structure stipulates
that only two thousand citizen signatures are
necessary to confirm parliamentary decisions
on a referendum. We therefore worked with
a multitude of commissions, each responsible
for a specific subject and representing residents, property owners, investors, experts,
and politicians. Integrating neighborhood
organizations into the process was an important consideration as well. The urban concept
for the Gundeldinger neighborhood, behind
the train station, evolved out of this collaboration. Finally, another important collaboration was with the media. We sought partners
among the local dailies and radio stations.
The local commercial radio station proved
a good ally. The studio was located across the
street from my apartment and I was able
to repeatedly present the project within the
context of local news. Armed with a slide
show, I attended over forty events during a

period of two years until political consensus
was finally reached on the urban concept
for the railway station area.

The urban concept for Basel's Saint Alban
Valley evolved out of a very different situation.
The city owned the most important building
lots in the area. Yet it had ceded all building
rights for these lots to the Christoph Merian
Foundation, a non-profit institution mandated to redevelop the historic neighborhood.
Within the building rights transaction, the city
and the foundation had agreed on a strategy
for urban renewal. The director of the foundation and I became the representatives of
the two parties. Together, we were property
owners, neighbors, investors, and political
representatives. This led to a very elitist
procedure. The urban concept evolved out of
the consensus reached during numerous
conversations in the area's local pub. We had
no need for a plan – it was in our heads.

In the case of the Luzernerring, a coherent
urban concept was first developed by a work
group of architects. The search for suitable
projects was then realized through open
competitions with a limited number of architects. From among the applicants, the jury
selected eight firms for the five building areas,
and via competition, chose the architects who
would be charged with executing the projects.
The jury was composed of the area's
investors, municipal representatives, and
independent experts.

The paths that led to the Owerri and Kunming
urban concepts were extremely different. As
I wrote earlier, I was not successful in creating
a dialogue about the gestalt of Owerri's very
particular cultural situation. This may have
been related to the conditions of the time, but
also may have resulted from the fact that
I was not yet forty, an important qualification,
according to Sir Patrick Abercrombie, for successful urban planning. [95]
The expectation in Owerri was that I, as the
lone expert, would show the way. When, three
months after having received the commission,
I first presented the concept's broad outlines

to the governor, it was approved a mere one hour after my presentation. The chief engineer of Imo State and I were asked to drive through the countryside to determine the location of important new streets and identify which houses would have to be demolished. Even in the later stages, cultural discourse occurred only with regard to details such as the location of the football stadium or access to the residential neighborhood for governmental ministers. My design for this residential district, incidentally, was described as a mousetrap. Since it only included one exit – very undesirable in certain political situations – it had to be altered to include three exits, as seen on page 156.

The process was yet again utterly different in Kunming. Upon searching for a unified urban concept, we found ourselves acting either as sparring partners or coaches for the municipal planning office. Since I had just turned fifty-six, I was qualified for the role. And in the eyes of the authorities and administration of Kunming, we were partners in a joint dialogue.

Modernism was characterized by linear processes led by an authority figure. The competition was the preferred tool for getting the most out of a project or concept. The anonymity of participants and openness of the process were the established rules of the game. This approach produced thousands of great buildings: the Sydney Opera House, the Centre Pompidou in Paris, the Congress Center in Lucerne, and Tegel Airport in Berlin. A competition with clear specifications sets the parameters. Participating architects retreat to their studios and search for the best solution. Then, without knowing which architect submitted which proposal, a jury selects a project for execution. This process has many advantages. It allows young architects to demonstrate their abilities. It makes it more difficult for the old boys' club to carry out backroom deals. Above all, however, it helps promote a creative and innovative search for the appropriate gestalt of the time. But the system also has its disadvantages.

Francesco Guardi's depiction of a competition design for the Ponte Rialto, Venice, 1750

The task's parameters must be very clearly defined to encourage submission of comparable projects. With urban design projects, this is not always possible and often not even desirable. Moreover, an architect's very crucial capacity for dialogue cannot be assessed in a competition.

The modernist obsession with the importance of individual objects, rather than the overall urban context, is receding into the background and a new consciousness and acceptance of the city's complexity is emerging in the beyond-the-modern period. Looking after the gestalt of the city means exploring the relationships between objects and harmonizing different themes and levels of the city. This brings urban issues into the foreground. At the same time, complex and contradictory situations require that the various parties within a city cooperate and collaborate in the search for solutions. Any method or process that does not take this into consideration has little chance for success.

Anonymous competitions can and should be used in cases where the partners have carefully discussed the project and clearly defined its final goal. At the same time, the project's anchoring in the site and configuration within the city must be free of fundamental contradictions. If this is not the case, it is sensible to choose other more open processes, which allow for dialogue about the complexity of the site.

During the past decades, alternative competition formats, such as involving several agencies in idea competitions, invitation-only competitions, multiphase competitions, and exploratory competitions, have been developed to respond to this need. But all these competitive formats do not respond radically to our beyond-the-modern needs. These demand a truly open collaboration between the different partners of the city and a fundamental openness in the discussion. Experimenting with more loosely defined procedures seems more promising in my view. These are variably referred to as test planning, workshops, or cooperative developmental planning.

LEUTSCHENBACH

Leutschenbach is an economically dynamic and spatially heterogeneous area in Zurich with tremendous potential for development. But the area appeared neglected. It showed considerable deficits, including zoning from an industrial past and a lack of traffic links within the urban district. The area measures approximately sixhundredthousand square meters, of which nearly half was owned by the city of Zurich. Important questions with regard to the area's identity, usage, urban design, open spaces, and traffic access had to be clarified.

To encourage investment, clear parameters had to be defined through an urban concept which would secure the spatial quality of the area. The Department of Building and Development described the process thus. "Due to the demanding situation and the many issues, the city of Zurich decided to follow a cooperative planning procedure. Together with planning teams, property owners, and city planning authorities, a general idea for the future area of Leutschenbach was developed through an open process. In contrast to an urban design competition, this process-oriented approach made it possible to tap into the pooled expertise of all participants and to openly discuss arising conflicts. The parameters and the task could thus be defined with precision in the course of the procedure. In collaboration with three planning teams, solutions were developed and actively discussed during three workshops. We used the following procedure. First, three different development strategies – called chance, center, and outskirt – were defined through test designs by the participating planning teams. From these three concepts, we derived two fundamentally different and detailed concepts. We called these mixed quarter and big city. The Leutschenbach urban concept resulted from these two development concepts." [96]

The Leutschenbach neighborhood on the northern edge
of Zurich

Third workshop in August 1998

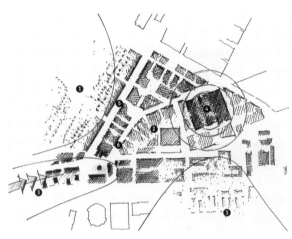

Urban concept for Leutschenbach
1 Integration of housing along the district boundaries; 2 Flexible mixed use
in middle area; 3 Dense development near Oerlikon train station; 4 Media
core with Swiss Television center; 5 Thurgauerstrasse as principal traffic
artery; 6 Leutschenbachstrasse as spine

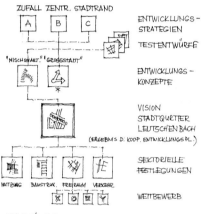

Procedural diagrams [97]

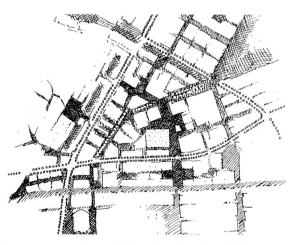

The open space concept serves to integrate the urban neighborhood
with the greater surrounding area.

THE URBAN ADVISORY
BOARD AS INSTITUTION

I believe that studying the political and administrative organizations specifically related to the beyond-the-modern city would be a worthwhile pursuit. Exploring these would probably lead to deliberations that go far beyond new public management issues. In this context, deliberation and action that depart from linear, and primarily object-focused thinking, are of primary interest. Reorienting the city planning office's focus to urbanism is one of the specific challenges of this new situation. The traditional organization of urban administration needs to be modified and should also include the creation of new institutions. For now, I limit my deliberations to one fairly new institution.

"Should a house be allowed to look like a dog?" Headline from a *SonntagsZeitung* article, November 7, 1993

The urban advisory board is a progressive institution for a new type of beyond-the-modern public management. It makes the city's gestalt the focus of public discourse, allows multiple voices to be heard, and is not based in law but in a city's culture. The prerequisite is that the council must not be abused as an ideological tool for elitist thinking. Basel's urban advisory board, made up of consulting architects, was nearly abolished by the city's government for this reason. The board can therefore only operate effectively if it is solidly anchored in the political system. The potential of the urban design advisory board's activities is not maximized unless it can rely on visions and urban concepts as a basis for transforming the city.

Basel's urban design advisory board is called a design commission; Zurich calls it a building committee; Salzburg and Halle call it an advisory board. I like the term advisory board for two reasons. The quest for quality within cities is not only related to its visual or aesthetic quality. It is equally important whether its gestalt is the expression of the identity and character of its inhabitants. Moreover, a city's gestalt is not transformed by committee or by assembling experts in order to assess the quality of projects. It is done through consultation – but in a dual understanding of the word: consultation as advice, meeting, exchange of opinions, and assessment; and consultation in the sense of providing support to city authorities in their quest for quality. This responsibility is not adequately expressed through the terms design commission or building committee.

In Basel, all building proposals are submitted to the urban design advisory board. In Salzburg, only projects of a certain scale are submitted to the advisory board. The rest of its members are foreigners. In Bremen, we were asked to only comment on urban design projects.

In Cologne, I remain the first and only non-local to sit on the urban design advisory board. In Salzburg, there was only one local member. The majority of the members were foreigners. In Germany's Halle on the Saale, none of the advisory board members live or work in the city. With the exception of myself, they all come from an area between Berlin and Dresden.

Due to constitutional law, in Germany, urban design advisory boards may only act as consultants. In Basel and Salzburg, the city's administration is bound by the decisions of the urban design advisory board. In Salzburg, appeals are made to the city council, and in Basel, to the administrative court. I am convinced that legal and political status is not important when the advisory board operates respectfully and diligently. During the six years that I chaired the urban design advisory board for the Austrian city of Feldkirch, the political authority responsible for building permits accepted all our recommendations.

In Salzburg and Halle, urban design advisory board meetings are open to the public, as long as the client does not expressly object. In Basel, Feldkirch, and Cologne, the sessions are held behind closed doors. In Cologne, even the client and architect are excluded from the consultation.

FELDKIRCH

Small projects often spark lengthy debates. Should the local contractor be allowed to build his dream villa? Does form that breaks with the rules of convention ruin uniformity or add color to the banality of a residential neighborhood? I believe the latter to be true. But my colleagues on the Feldkirch urban design advisory board disagreed and the dream villa was never realized. Still, we were all in agreement when asked to approve a sort of dream-castle proposal for the redevelopment of the existing Rösslepark pub. The proposed design was outdated and pseudo-romantic. We requested an architectural competition in order to arrive at a more contemporary solution. [96]

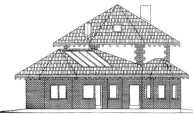

The Dream Villa: interfering with uniformity or enriching through variety?

First building submission for redeveloping the Rösslepark pub...

...and the actual solution

BASEL

The owner of the existing building at Allschwilerstrasse 90 in Basel wanted to tear it down, despite the fact that it showed superior quality both in urban design and architecture. The urban design advisory commission decided the building could only be torn down if its replacement was equally exceptional. We believed this should be achieved through an architectural competition. Among the competition entries, Herzog & de Meuron's proposal delivered this quality and we approved the demolition.

The former Schwitter Printers building on Basel's Allschwilerstrasse

One of the Basel urban design advisory commission's established rules is that projects developed through competitions can no longer be questioned. There are times, however, when this can misfire. I had insisted that the Union Bank of Switzerland should have a competition for the design of its new building. The client wanted to leave its mark on the urban landscape in a very autonomous manner. The bank thought that a prominent architect from Southern Switzerland's Ticino area seemed the ideal choice. To ensure that he would be selected in the competion, the client even invited another architect from Ticino to sit on the jury. As a result, each remark by jury members critisizing the "autistic savings box" was drowned out by both the client and the architect's colleague from Ticino.

The Herzog & de Meuron building chosen in competition

Bank building on Basel's Aeschenplatz, designed by Lugano, Switzerland architect Mario Botta

HALLE

A historic building on the German city's central market square was to be torn down to facilitate construction of a new department store. To preserve the city's historic character and prevent the square from becoming stale and commonplace, the advisory board recommended the denial of this request. It claimed that by destroying the historic building, the department store would drastically reduce the variety of the square's urban design and become an excessively dominant element. Following an intensive public debate, the city council agreed to adopt our recommendation.

The municipal land office had sold property on a tributary of the Saale River to an investor without any conditions. The investor planned two riverside residences. The project would cut across the riverside promenade and stand out aggressively in the neighborhood. To achieve a better solution, the advisory board recommended a competition among four architects. The property owner agreed and ended up with a far more attractive solution.

Construction of a department store on the market square in Halle on the Saale without demolition of the existing Marktplatz 22 structure...

...and with demolition of the historic building

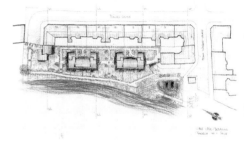

The first disjointed design proposal...

...and the second design solution, integrated into the fabric of the city

SALZBURG

The public bidding process for the architectural contract for the Salzburg Festival's new festival hall was manipulated by the state's government so that architect Wilhelm Holzbauer received the commission. The Salzburg advisory board, however, described Holzbauer's project as "the worst ever submitted," and recommended its rejection. The jury had even twice chosen other architects. As expected, these recommendations had little effect. Mafia-style deal-making within the state government proved a much stronger tool of persuasion than any endorsement – or lack thereof – provided by the board.

SAMSTAG, 7. DEZEMBER 2002

IM WIDERSPRUCH:
Jean Baudrillard über
Terrorismus heute
IM GLÜCK:
Was macht Christiane
mit der Million?
Seiten 4 & 5

DER STANDARD
ALBUM

IM GEBÄLK:
Peter Handke
zum Sechzigsten
IN ALLER SCHNELLE:
Espressomaschinen
im Test
Seiten 8 & 14

Eine Tribüne, auf der man die Herrscher im Land der architektonischen Un-Demokratie huldvoll hutzwedelt und auf das fleck im ersten handwedeln sehen darf: das große Balkon an der Stoßfassade des Holzbauer-Entwurfs. Im Bild unten: die Innenraum-Sit.

Ein Balkon ward geboren

Weil die Salzburger Festspiele selbst dazu nicht in der moralischen Lage waren, stellt nun die Initiative Architektur Salzburg alle Projekte des Verfahrens Kleines Festspielhaus aus und würzt die Schau mit einer „Chronologie der Ereignisse".
Von Ute Woltron.

Nein, es war keine Premiere, so weit wollen wir in unserer Reseonon gut nicht gehen. Es war vielmehr ein Schaustück in vielen schillernden Akten, ein Possentheater uhne Tradition, das man wohrlich noch nicht untergegangen glauben darf...

Plötzlich alles anders

Carl Fingerhuth über die böswillige Verführung naiver Volljähriger

Ich war auch einer der naiven Volljährigen. Vier Jahre lang hatte ich im Gestaltungsbeirat der Stadt Salzburg verantwortungsvolle Kulturpolitik zu Gunsten architektonischer und städtebaulicher Qualität erlebt; mit einem engagierten Stadtrat, der uns zuhörte und auch anspruchsvolle Entscheidungen mittrug; mit einer Verwaltung, die immer wieder genaue Formulierungen verlangte und einer Öffentlichkeit, die an Transparenz gewöhnt war. Vertrauensvoll ließ ich mich in ein Beurteilungsgremium wählen, das vom Land Salzburg gebildet worden war – naiv wie ich war. Wir sollten das Kuratorium der Salzburger Festspiele bei seiner Suche nach einem Projekt für den Neubau des kleinen Festspielhauses unterstützen.

Fünf Architekten aus drei Ländern wurden ausgesucht. In kürzester Frist sollten sie ein Projekt für eine außerordentlich anspruchsvolle Aufgabe ausarbeiten. Die Projekte wurden dem Beurteilungsgremium vorgelegt. Es empfahl einstimmig das Projekt der Arbeitsgemeinschaft Hermann & Valentiny/Wimmer-Zaic.

Dann kam aber plötzlich alles anders. Es begann eine für einen Naiven unglaubliche und unfassbare Serie von politischen Machenschaften und Manipulationen.

– Der ehrenwerte Architekt Holzbauer, der nur auf dem zweiten Platz gelandet war, deponierte beim Bundesvergabeamt einen Einspruch gegen das erstplatzierte Projekt. Dabei verfügte er offensichtlich über detaillierte Informationen zum erstplatzierten Projekt, die nur beim Land Salzburg zu finden waren.

– Es wurde vom Vertreter des Landeshauptmanns der Antrag gestellt, wegen der Verstöße der Erstplatzierten den ehrenwerten Architekten auf dem zweiten Platz mit der Bearbeitung des Projektes zu beauftragen, obwohl dessen Projekt auch voll von Verstößen war.

– Nachdem diese Aktion nicht erfolgreich war, wurde eine Neubeurteilung angeordnet und vorgenommen. Damit diese Aktion sicher zu Gunsten des ehrenwerten Architekten ausgehen würde, wurden die „Spielregeln" geändert. Jetzt sollten auch Arbeitsgemeinschaften zwischen den eingeladenen Architekten zulässig sein. Die Erstplatzierten wurden massiv unter Druck gesetzt, sich mit dem ehrenwerten Architekten zusammen zu schließen. Valentiny hat mir gesagt, er hätte in diesem Zusammenhang, unter vielen anderen Pressionen, einen Anruf der Außenministerin seines Heimatlandes Luxemburg erhalten.

– In der Vorprüfung durch das Amt der Landesregierung wurden die nicht eingehaltenen feuerpolizeilichen Vorschriften des ehrenwerten Architekten nicht erwähnt. Das hätte zu einer massiven Reduktion der Sitzplatzzahlen geführt und damit die gerühmte Wirtschaftlichkeit des Projektes zerstört.

– Zur Sicherheit wurde bei der zweiten Beurteilung aus formellen Gründen zuerst einmal das Projekt von Wimmer ausgeschieden, der das Fusionsspiel nicht mitgemacht und ein eigenes Projekt eingegeben hatte.

– Leider führte aber auch die Neubeurteilung durch das Beurteilungsgremium nicht zum „richtigen" Resultat. Dieses empfahl nämlich mit deutlichem Vorsprung das Projekt von Bétrix und Consolascio zur Ausführung. So musste zum sechsten Mal die Trickkiste aktiviert werden. Über ein Gutachten eines Tiefbauingenieurs wurde das Urteil des Beurteilungsgremiums umgestoßen und der ehrenwerte Architekt auf den ersten Platz gesetzt. Im Beurteilungsgremium war kein Tiefbauingenieur vertreten, dafür aber Theaterfachleute, die Vertreter von Stadt und Land, die Sachverständigenkommission für Altstadterhaltung, die Mitglieder des Kuratoriums der Salzburger Festspiele und unabhängige und neutrale Berater.

Der Verlauf des Verfahrens enthält eine Vielzahl von gravierenden Tatbeständen, die mich zutiefst verunsichern.

– Eine demokratisch legitimierte Landesregierung täuscht ein Konkurrenzverfahren vor, lässt vier Architekten zweimal mehrere zehntausend Euros investieren, hat aber von Anfang an die feste Absicht, nur ihren ehrenwerten Freund zu beauftragen. In meinem Rechtsverständnis ist das arglistige Täuschung.

– Sie verwendet dazu ein Verfahren, das in Europa geschaffen wurde, um „mafiose" Praktiken bei der Vergabe von öffentlichen Aufträgen zu verunmöglichen. Damit diskreditiert sie den Kampf gegen die korrupte Verknüpfung von Politik und wirtschaftlichen Interessen und setzt sich selber diesem Vorwurf aus.

– Das Prinzip der Konkurrenzverfahren ist eines der wichtigsten Instrumente, um in der Stadt bei architektonischen und städtebaulichen Aufgaben soziale, ökonomische und kulturelle Qualität entstehen zu lassen. Es ist auch das wichtigste Instrument, um jungen Architekten eine Chance zu geben, sich gegen das ergraute und verfilzte Establishment zu profilieren. So sind in Venedig der Rialto (schon vor mehreren Jahrhunderten), in Paris das Centre Pompidou und in London die neue Tate Gallery entstanden. Das Verfahren um das Salzburger Festspielhaus ist in dieser Sicht eine kulturelle Katastrophe.

Zuletzt eine persönliche Bemerkung. Nach der zweiten Diskreditierung der Teilnehmer und des Beurteilungsgremiums hatte ich eigentlich erwartet, dass dieser Entscheid in Salzburg und Österreich eine öffentliche Diskussion in Gang setzen würde. Als Ausländer fühlte ich mich nicht legitimiert, die politische und kulturelle Situation zu kommentieren. Ich habe jetzt diesen Beitrag trotzdem geschrieben, weil ich den Eindruck hatte, dass dieser erschreckende Vorgang bei vielen meiner österreichischen Freunde gar nicht wahrgenommen worden ist.

Carl Fingerhuth, wohnhaft in Zürich, ist an der ETH diplomierter Architekt und Honorarprofessor der Technischen Universität Darmstadt. Er war Mitglied des Salzburger Gestaltungsbeirates von 1997 bis 2001.

Response by the press to the Salzburg Festival's new festival hall,
Der Standard, December 7, 2002. Translation see p. 206-207 [99]

"Wrapped in veils as protection from swarming bees, Raji girls watch a hunter gathering honey high above in a tree." [100]

—

AND I AM BEGINNING TO KNOW THE MAP, THE DIRECTIONS.

__ *Dag Hammarskjöld, second Secretary General of the United Nations, diary entry on August 24, 1961, one month before his death.* [101]

FENG SHUI

PREMISE:
CONSCIOUSNESS OF MAN'S HARMONY
WITH THE UNIVERSE SHOULD BE
INTEGRATED INTO THE GESTALT OF
THE CITY.

The civilized arts, according to ancient Chinese lore, were introduced by the country's first emperor, Fu-Hsi. "The sage looks up to heaven and … he observes all the celestial phenomena, he contemplates the earth and … examines the outlines of the ground."[102] This is the origin of the Chinese science of *feng shui*. The heavenly constellations are reflected in the landscape, the interests of the living are brought into harmony with those of the dead, and the cosmic influence on human concerns is activated. The literal translation of *feng shui* is "wind and water." According to Taoist philosophy, *feng shui* is "a thing like wind, which you cannot comprehend, and like water, which you cannot grasp."[103]

In 1873, the British missionary E. J. Eitel published the first book written by a European about *feng shui*. In the conclusion he describes *feng shui* as the "foolish daughter of a wise mother."[104] When, in the course of working on the concept for northern Kunming, I inquired about this wise mother notion, I received such confusing answers as, "It helps to gain acceptance among old people." Nevertheless there are many hints of *feng shui*'s deeper

rootedness in the culture. Even in 1979, "superstitious" practices like *feng shui* were still expressly forbidden in the Criminal Code of the People's Republic of China. Evidently, ancient energy remains present and retains its influence on political decisions.

Equipped with our modern ways of thinking, we don't quite know how to deal with *feng shui*. We must take the mental detour recommended by François Jullien in *Detour and Access*. Without it, our fascination centers on *feng shui*'s foolish daughter, which in turn seduces us into playing foolish games. It seems that much of what is published today in the West under the heading of *feng shui* bears little connection to its original content and meaning. With Jullien's detour, we can try making contact with the wise mother again. I am convinced that her power and importance are linked to the rediscovery of our inner self in the present day.

Superficially, the wise mother is manifest in our time in our desire for sustainable development. We are searching for an attitude that corresponds to the needs of the present time without endangering the opportunities of future generations. This has led to the expression, on many different levels, of a multitude of technical and organizational measures related to caring for cities. The range of these measures is extremely wide. The Rio U.N. Conference's Agenda 21, which calls for the careful integration of the individual citizen into the planning process, is characterized by this approach. So too is the Kyoto Protocol, which demands a drastic reduction in carbon monoxide air pollution and includes such pioneers of low-tech building as Hassan Fathy and Paolo Soleri, and superstar of high-tech architecture Norman Foster, who claims his high-rises adhere to the latest ecological standards. It seems to me that this is more a case of the wise mother's crazy daughter guiding the designer's computer mouse.

Basel's Breite bathing spot on the Rhine river, designed by architects Andreas Scheiwiller and Matthias Oppliger, is an example of sustainable development. "The *Rheinbad Breite*, threatened with demolition, was preserved through a reduction in scale – which also reduced operating costs – in keeping with the wishes of local residents. The bathing station on the river is considered environmentally friendly because its operation requires hardly any energy resources."[105]

The Swiss Re Tower, an example of sustainable development in London, designed by architect Norman Forster and dubbed "the gherkin" by locals. The foolish daughter of a wise mother?

Philosopher Gernot Böhme, in his book about aesthetics as a universal theory of perception, writes about an entirely different ecology. "The threatening deterioration of nature as environment, concern about natural resources, and personal experiences of the damage inflicted upon nature, lead to a questioning of nature – yet the subject is no longer nature itself. This critique has inspired the demand for an ecological aesthetic of nature. This aesthetic complements the ecological approach – which remains purely scientific and addresses human needs only on a physiological level – and deals with nature in terms of its meaning for humankind. The relationship between environmental qualities and the human condition form the basis for an ecological aesthetic of nature. If this aesthetic dimension of ecology were to be developed, reproduction and future management in the form of reclaiming and re-cultivating natural environments that have already been destroyed, would no longer focus simply on creating functional eco-systems and interesting biotopes. Instead, it would be dedicated to creating a humane environment."[106]

This takes us back to *feng shui*. Taoists see themselves as part of the cosmos, part of heaven and earth. In 1873, Eitel wrote in *Feng Shui: The Rudiments of Natural Science in China*, that the Confucians, "look upon nature not as a dead inanimate fabric, but as a living breathing organism. They see a golden chain of spiritual life running through every form of existence and binding together, as in one living body, everything that subsists in heaven above or on earth below."[107] *Feng shui* refers to an unbroken consciousness of the harmony between humankind and nature. Since people are a part of the cosmos, there can be no distance or separation from nature. On the other hand, humans have a responsibility to fit into the game of forces and to observe its laws.

"The southwestern paradise of
the Padmasambhava"

A geomancer in the late Ch'ing dynasty uses
his compass to divine the characteristics of a
potential building site.

Chinese culture integrated and formalized
our responsibility and knowledge of the
energetic qualities of space and time and the
hidden forces of the earth, [108] like no other.
"Achieve the harmony of the Middle, and
Heaven and Earth will be in their right place,
and all things will flourish," instructs the
Li-chi, the Book of Rites. The importance of geomantic principles in China is rooted in this
cosmic understanding of its culture. Contrary
to Christian, Hindu, and Buddhist religions,
Chinese spirituality is not focused on space
and time beyond the here and now. Thus,
Chinese religion is not a religion but rather
a philosophy of interacting with sensual experiences; with stones, plants, animals, people,
wind, and water. [109]

The principles of Chinese geomancy are:
– Heaven and earth are connected.
– A constant flux of energy (chi) between
  heaven and earth makes transformations
  possible. The energy flows along the
  dragon veins.
– Macrocosm and microcosm correspond
  to one another.
– Energy flows from sky to earth, from north
  to south, from top to bottom. The best sites
  have mountains behind them and water
  in front of them.

Man is a part of nature, not separate from it.
"The world (the cosmos) is thus harmonious.
It is not static. The transformation (yi), the
forces of yin and yang, the five elements of
the transformational phases, make the world
into a 'process'," [110] writes Roman Malek.
Humankind should not subjugate the earth,
but live in the world (Tao) with care and mindfulness (wu wei), deal with it in a respectful
and virtuous manner (te), and be conscious
that everything is in flux (yin and yang). To be
able to do so, humankind must gain excellent
knowledge of the world. Because of this perspective, Chinese culture has a long tradition
of studying nature and developing the necessary technical tools to do so. The Chinese
invented the magnetic compass, for instance,
long before Europeans did.

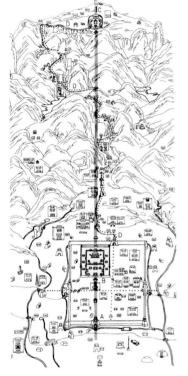

Tai Shan, the sacred mountain of
the East in Shandong and the city of Tai'an.
Eighteenth-century depiction

In *Taoism: The Quest for Immortality*, John
Blofeld writes: "Since pure *yang*, also known
as cosmic *yang*, pertains to heaven and pure
or cosmic *yin* refers to the earth, there has
to be a means for them to commingle. It is
taught that, at certain places, there are 'dragon
veins', that is to say invisible lines running
down from the sky into the mountains and
along the earth, whose function is rather
similar to that of psychic channels within the
human body which play such an important
part in acupuncture and in yoga, whether
Chinese, Indian or Tibetan ... The situating of
new dwellings and of graves is determined
in accordance with this science, so as to take
maximum advantage of the inflow of cosmic
vitality and to ensure a correct balance of
yin and *yang*." [111] The desired harmony found
its gestalt by depending on local topography,
wrote Needham, "since every place had
features of landscape that would modify the
local influences of the various *chhi* [sic]
of nature. The shapes of hills and valleys, the
directions of streams and rivers, being the
outcome of 'winds and waters', were the most
important." [112]

At the beginning of the workshop to develop
an urban concept for Kunming's northward
expansion, I asked to have the parameters
defined. Our Chinese partners replied without
hesitation. There were only two elements we
needed to take into consideration: aside from
the preexisting highway, we had to respect
the *feng shui* line that ran from a hill to the
north to the great axis of the existing city.

In the West, modernism predicated a very
different understanding of our relationship
with the cosmos. An impregnable boundary
lies between the human body and its soul and
also between humankind and nature. Therefore, we must, writes Malek, "make a great
effort to relate to this traditional Chinese
sense of the world. We are so used to seeing
the physical world as something 'outside of
us,' as a generally hostile environment, or as
purely material matter (to be exploited), that
we can barely grasp the Chinese sense of
unity with the universe. Man is a part of this

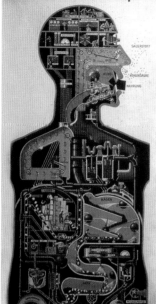

The human body as a machine without a soul, as illustrated in a German school poster from the 1950s

unity, only a part, but a true part. Chinese man traditionally sees himself as a being who, although just one manifestation among many in the world, must face others with respect and without any desire to rule over them ... Following nature, allowing oneself to be influenced by it, guiding it at most ... cultivating it and giving it ritual order – this is the ideal Chinese attitude born out of this view of the world. One can only understand it as a transfer of universal norms onto the human and societal dimension." [113]

We would build entirely different cities today if these ideas were linked and integrated into our thinking. The relationship between cities and landscapes, and between man and nature, takes on vital importance in terms of the gestalt of our cities.

Alan Watts' introduction to Taoism does not include *feng shui*. His focus was on the transformation of human consciousness rather than the transformation of cities. In his time, consciousness about the relationship between humankind and the earth was only just taking shape. I am convinced that this relationship is as important today as the awareness of the polarity of all existence. It is one of the great philosophical themes to continuously captivate humankind through-out the evolution of its consciousness. Yet when we remained obsessed with our own rational potential, there was no place for it.

The Chinese were not the only ones to develop this consciousness. Sensing the special qualities of a specific place was an ability shared by pre-modern people around the world. Readers of Carlos Castaneda may remember his account of his first meeting with his spiritual teacher, Don Juan. One evening, Castaneda arrives at Don Juan's house for the first time. Don Juan tells him to spend the night outside on the porch. His first task is to find the perfect spot to sleep. This task occupies him all night long. [114]

Similarly, the survival of prehistoric hunters and gatherers often depended on assessing the pros and cons of various sites. As people became settled in one spot, they lost this ability. Yet depending on the cultural perspective, geomantic knowledge remains present. We call on it when seeking favorable living conditions, as a tool in agricultural production, as a spiritual link to the cosmos, or as an instrument used by gurus to exercise power.

Before exploring geomancy's connection to beyond-the-modern urbanism, it seems useful to show how its practice informed city gestalt since ancient times. The goal in doing so, however, is not to figure out how to integrate the forms and structures of a bygone consciousness, but rather to explore how knowledge about the quality of a space can be applied to what we know, and deal with, today.

Killing mosquitoes with DDT in Jones Beach State Park, New York, 1945

ORDERING THE CITY
BEFORE MODERNISM

ORDERING THE CITY ACCORDING
TO THE CONSTELLATIONS

From very early on, the gestalt of the city
was defined by information gleaned from
observing the constellations. I suspect that by
doing this, humans wanted to demonstrate,
on a worldly level, their consciousness of the
unity of mankind to the cosmos. As a physical
expression of their anchoring in the universe,
early cities were arranged according to astronomical discoveries.

Positioning in Basel

Each morning, when I still lived in an apartment in Basel, my bedroom window framed a
rectangle of sunlight on the wall. As the sun
began to rise over the course of the morning,
the rectangle slowly moved across the wall.
For an entire summer, I started my morning
by outlining this rectangle on my wall with
a black pencil. The following year, I adopted a
more precise approach. Since I was living
according to the very regular schedule of a
civil servant at that time, I used a red pencil
to trace the window's outline on my wall each
morning at exactly quarter past seven. A pin
with a red head marked the upper left-hand
corner of the window for each sunny day.

By springtime, the rectangle was in the
upper right-hand corner of the wall. Then it
wandered lower and further to the left with
each passing day. At the same hour, the sun
stood higher and further north. On the longest
day and shortest night, summer solstice,
the sun turned and the field of light began
migrating toward the right. Having studied
this in school, I was not overly surprised. Yet
I was startled by the sun's trajectory, marked
with a red pin in each successive tracing. The
sun was not returning along the same line.

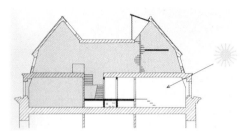

My apartment in Basel

My bedroom wall...

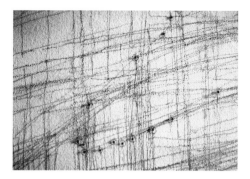

...with the summer end of the lemniscate charting the annual
course of the sun

It curved downward and only crossed the upper line on the autumn solstice. Seen from afar, the pins appeared to have evolved into a reclining figure eight – an ancient symbol for infinity and the eternal rhythm.

The Celtic Raurici tribe surely observed the sky above Basel in a similar fashion more than two thousand years ago, consciously registering the rhythms of the sun and incorporating them into their city. They integrated their knowledge of the world with their *buan*, the way they wanted to be on earth. They wanted to express themselves with an urban concept defined by the constellations.

A first geomantic system is evident in the naming of mountain peaks which, after nearly two thousand years, bear the same Celtic-based names. Rolf d'Aujourdhui, a former archaeologist for Basel and its surroundings, wrote about the city's geomantic position in the context of sun and moon. "Seen from the French Ballon d'Alsace, the sun rises on the longest day (June 24) exactly above the Petit Ballon; at the start of spring (May 1st) above the Grand Ballon; on the solstices (March 21 and September 21) above Germany's Ballon of Baden; and on the shortest day (December 21) above Switzerland's Ballon of the Jura. Three other mountains with the same name, the blue mountains – the Swiss Blue Mountain, the Blue Mountain of Baden, and the High Blue Mountain – are linked to the extreme positions of the moon in the cycle of this planet which takes 18.5 years. The origin of Basel lies precisely at the point where a sun line (Petit Ballon and Ballon of the Jura Mountain) intersects a moon line (Blue Jura Mountains and Blue Mountains of Baden). Thus Basel is the ideal center point of the zone surrounded by the three Ballons." [115]

In tarot cards, the lemniscate as horizontal figure eight is an ancient symbol for the eternal rhythm of life

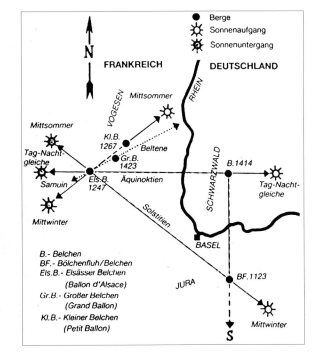

The Belchen Triangle

The orientation of a Celtic cult site – subsequently the site of a Christian cathedral – and the positioning of the street leading to it, provide another example of Celtic geomantic practice. On solstice days, the effects of this orientation can still be experienced. At sunrise, a shaft of light enters precisely through the front cathedral window. At a perfect right angle to this shaft of light lies a Celtic road, whose surface was uncovered during several excavations. This road leads directly from the cathedral hill to the St. Johann Quarter and onward, far into the Alsace. The city's "landscape (at that time) was the dial of a topographical-astronomical clock," writes d'Aujourdhui.

The Celtic axis on the Münsterplatz...

...and in the St. Johann district

Positioning in Giza

The base corners of the Great Pyramid of Cheops – whose sides measure two-hundred meters – and those of Chephren, and Mycerinus as well, are each nearly perfectly level. Also each is carefully positioned toward the cardinal points with equal precision. Inside Cheops, shafts lead from the king' and queen's chambers to the outside. A variety of technical and functional explanations have been suggested to explain the existence of these shafts. My personal opinion is that the explanation lies in the connection between astronomy and spirituality. This interpretation is based on the astronomical alignment of the shafts with the heavenly constellations around 2500 BC when Cheops was built. The southern shaft departing from the king's chamber points precisely to the Orion constellation's highest point at that time. Orion was the celestial representation of Osiris, who played an important role as the god of resurrection and rebirth. [116] Cheops is thus not only rooted in the rhythm of time, but also in its linear progression.

Positioning in Beijing

China's astrology is closely linked to natural philosophy. Richard Wilhelm, German translator of the *I Ching*, writes: "Heaven, Earth and Man are the three forces in the world, and it is man who has to bring the other two – Heaven, the creative force of temporal events, and Earth, the receptive force of spatial expansion – into harmony. Heaven shows the images, the destined man realizes them. The Book of Changes (*I Ching*), which contains this sentence, is based on the knowledge that static conditions are not the ultimate reality, but the spiritual law from which every occurrence receives its meaning and the impulse of lasting effect."

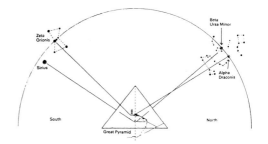

Astronomical alignment of the four shafts of the Great Pyramid of Cheops dating back to around 2500 BC

The three pyramids at Giza

The central axis of Beijing's Imperial Palace

The positioning of Beijing's Imperial Palace was defined in 1406 BC. Its principal axis points exactly north to south. Along this axis, artificial landscape creates the exact spatial characteristics recommended by *feng shui*. To the north, an artificial mountain links the earth with the sky and ensures lasting continuity in the cosmos. To the south, winding bodies of water illustrate the vitality of terrestrial life.

Positioning in Stonehenge

The monumental stone circle of Stonehenge is located in southern England. It was erected between 3100 and 1100 BC. The oldest sections of Stonehenge, the Aubrey Holes, are cavities in the ground arranged in a circle that measures eighty-seven meters in diameter. One theory suggests that their purpose is to calculate, by shifting poles between the holes, the time of solar and lunar eclipses. This assumes knowledge of the exact length of the solar year down to two decimals, or 365.25 days. Again, I cannot prove whether this explanation is correct, but it makes sense to me in principle. There is no doubt, however, that the massive stones were positioned according to astronomical occurrences.

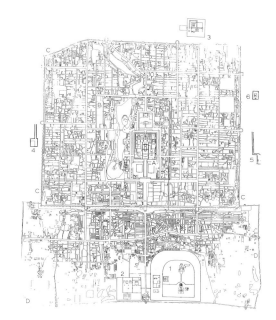

Beijing's Forbidden City

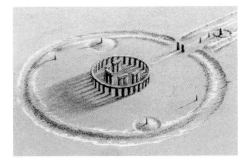

Reconstruction of England's Stonehenge as it might have appeared around 1500 BC

Sunset at Stonehenge

ORDERING CITIES BASED ON SACRED TERRITORIES

It seems that all civilizations on this planet are "shown images in the sky, which the destined man realizes" in the mythical era. This was first manifested when cities were positioned according to celestial constellations. Around the world, city spatial order began to display, through use of the square, a similar pattern for its two-dimensional organization. Once again, an archetypal structure for the city evolved around the globe.

The Chinese City as Square

"It is said that Heaven is round and the Earth is square. Is that true? The square is dark and the round is bright. When *yin* and *yang* are in the places that are fitting to them, tranquility and peace reign ... Heaven provides the spiritual concept, man brings order and organization to things."

These quotes from ancient Chinese manuscripts refer to archetypal forms in which the square is a symbol of the earth, and the circle a symbol of heaven. The Chinese mandala is also based on the concept of a round heaven and a square earth. The mandala develops from the inside out, alternating through concentric circles and squares, beginning and ending either in the square (order and knowledge of man), or in the circle (chaos and reality of nature). The geometrical game between circle and square is based on the idea that heaven, earth, and humankind are in precise relation to one another. As described in the *Book of Customs*, written during the Han dynasty, the square is therefore the basic pattern for order and organization within the city. The motif of the square is repeated as in a holarchic system. The country's capital is a square composed of nine squares. The altar of the ancestors is located to the left (east), the altar of the earth to the right (west), guests are received in the foreground, and the market takes place in the background. This pattern was employed as far back as the end of the second millennium BC, in the plan for the royal city of Zhangzhou.

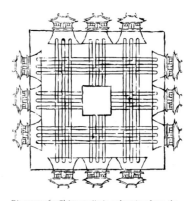

Diagram of a Chinese city in a drawing from the first century BC

Khara Khoto, China

This diagram was used as a basis for planning Chinese cities right up until the twentieth century. As part of an annual spring ritual, the emperor performed the role of "first farmer" and ploughed the city's inner square, known as the sacred square. There are indications that this pattern may have originated from the agricultural division of fields, where the center field was a public field cultivated by all the owners of the other eight fields. The yield from the center parcel of land was handed over to the dignitaries. The diagram of the nine fields is also said to have influenced the division of the empire into nine provinces under the legendary Yü the Great, the founder of China's first dynasty.

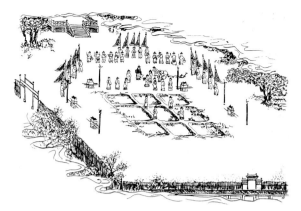

A seventeenth-century depiction of the emperor ploughing the sacred field in front of the altar of agriculture in Beijing

The Roman City as Square

Quite fascinatingly, similar images defined the foundations of Roman cities. A square is laid out, positioned precisely facing northward, fixed with axes, and spiritually anchored with a ritual corresponding closely to the Chinese emperor's springtime plowing of the sacred field. According to Plutarch, the ritual was based on Etruscan ceremonial books. These stipulated that a pit filled with sacrificial offerings and soil from the fields, called *mundus*, would mark the sacred center of a settlement. The plowing of a sacred furrow would ban evil from the boundaries of the settlement and separate it from the surrounding countryside.

The first furrow, the *sulcus primigenius*, is ploughed. Roman relief from Aquileia

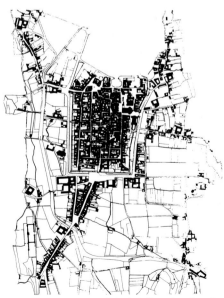

The Roman urban plan is still clearly visible in the cadastral survey of Como from 1858.

The Aztec City as Square

In *The City Shaped: Urban Patterns and Meanings Through History*, Spiro Kostof writes: "Some urbanists have argued that ancient towns were shaped by symbolism rather than pragmatic logic. The mythical foundation of the Aztec capital Tenochtitlàn (later Mexico City) in the mid-fourteenth century is depicted in a page from the *Codex Mendoza*. At the intersection of four streams (recalling the four-part division of the city that remained well into the post-Conquest era), the location of the future capital is revealed through a sacred portent." [117]

The Aztec city of Tenochtitlàn in the *Codex Mendoza*

The urban plan of Mexico City in the foundation scroll from 1563

The Christian City as Square

The New Jerusalem is described in the Bible's book of Revelations, chapter 21. "And it had a wall great and high, and twelve gates ... On the east three gates; on the north three gates; on the south three gates; and on the west three gates ... and the city lieth foursquare, and the length is as large as the breadth." [118]

Titus Burckhardt, a scholar from Basel, writes, "The heavenly Jerusalem is in fact the 'squaring' of the heavenly cycle, its twelve gates corresponding to the twelve months of the year, as well as to the analogous divisions of the greater cycles, such as the precession of the equinoxes which, in the ancient world system, is the greatest of all the astronomical cycles and therefore the largest measure of time. The Apocalypse mentions 'twelve thousand furlongs' as the measure of the city's circuit; this number corresponds to the 'great year' of the Persians and is in fact an approximate measure for half the equinoxial cycle, namely for the time of the reversion of the equinoxes (12,960 years)." [119]

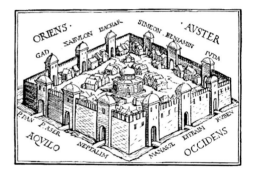

Woodcut by Hans Holbein, 1497–1543, depicting the new Jerusalem according to the book of Revelation

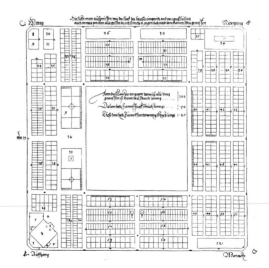

Various means of fortifying cities, castles, and market towns, Albert Dürer, 1527

The Indian City as Square

In Indian mythology, urban plans are depicted as reflections of the creation of the world. "The Indian building master was a descendent of the divine building master Visvakarna, who was born from one of the four faces of Brahma, the Creator of the World ... The unstructured cosmos, Vastu-Purusha, is forced into a specific form – namely a square – when Brahma lays the foundations for a city, and is kept in this form by the gods ... To the Veda, this square was a symbol of the immovable, timeless, and absolute gestalt of Vastu-Purusha in contrast to the circle, the symbol of the terrestrial world and the movement of time." [120] It is a compelling correspondence that the celestial abode of Vaikuntha has twelve gates, just like the new Jerusalem.

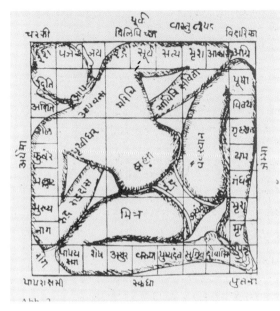

The hump-backed earth spirit Vastu Purushu is forced into a square shape.

The Vaikuntha paradise mandala, the heavenly home of Vishnu

FENG SHUI IN THE BEYOND-THE-MODERN ERA

This heading is somewhat misleading. Since the Middle Ages, cities were no longer planned and built in harmony with nature and the cosmos; on the contrary, nature became a threat that had to be controlled. The principles of city gestalt were increasingly governed by rational needs and goals. Military security became the overriding concern in establishing the boundaries of medieval cities and purely functional goals determined their internal structures.

The market areas, streets, and lanes were defined by separating public and private space. Private space was divided into lots in accordance with each individual citizen's space requirements. The goal was to create the best conditions for private investors. But the street also became a medium for demonstrating political power. It broadcast the beginning of a new era and directed the eye and the way toward public buildings. By the nineteenth century at the latest, the principal goal was to create a structure that allowed for unfettered growth. Finally, the need for unlimited automobile mobility became the defining criterion for structure.

Throughout these observations, I wish to draw attention once more to one of the fundamental premises of this book in relation to *feng shui*. Each era – in line with its social, economic, and cultural goals – defines a specific gestalt for its cities. Thus the pre-modern era reflected its spirituality in its cities. Modernism's exploration of rationality led to the suppression of spirituality and the gestalt of its cities was therefore shaped by rational energies. Sooner or later in the beyond-the-modern era, a new city gestalt will emerge as well, giving expression to the new energies of our times. Western spirituality is re-emerging with great force nowadays and is connected to our roles in the cosmos. This is creating a new relationship with the universe, to nature, and to landscape, or rather to what

Construction of palisades on the outskirts of Bremgarten, Switzerland, as illustrated in an image from a medieval chronicle

Los Angeles, USA

the Taoists describe as the "wind you cannot comprehend," and the "water you cannot grasp."

This experience of spiritual connectedness is evident in the newfound commitment to ecology-minded cities, in all their various forms. Yet while this movement is rooted in spirituality, its current outward manifestation remains, in practice, still technical. It deals with the management of land and existing structures, the reduction of environmental pollution, transportation and traffic policies, energy resource management, ecological water management, the protection and development of green spaces, and waste management. These issues are explored in depth elsewhere and I do not wish to re-explore their various uses and applications within urban planning, urban design, and architecture. Still, I believe little consideration has been given to the fundamental implications of our newfound spiritual connection to the cosmos beyond obvious ecological tasks. In this regard, we are only at the beginning of a great and long process.

What might *feng shui* mean on a new, consciously spiritual level? One thing is certain: we cannot fall back on pre-modern practices. They no longer correspond to the state of our consciousness. *Feng shui* would become a foolish game with outdated and formal rules. And yet the fundamental message of *feng shui* illuminates a path that could lead us out of the trap of only considering the technical aspects of projects. At the same time, we have to let go of dated romantic notions and instead look for solutions in the energies of today. The key is to transform the polarity between cities and nature into mutual respect. Thus nature, together with the city, can once again become the conscious basis for human existence, a partner that accepts us if we meet it with respect.

I would like to document several approaches that can lead us into the potential depth of this partnership and, hence, of the spiritual experience. From this place, the wise mother can give us pointers about how to rediscover harmony with nature. Perhaps it is time to adapt the Lord's Prayer for the beyond-the-modern age. We no longer need to be delivered from evil, but rather released from the bonds of too rational an understanding of the world.

RESPECTING LANDSCAPE

The early modern city separated itself from its natural surroundings with walls and ditches. Only farm settlements played along with nature's rules. The modern city abolished this differentiation and modern urban dwellers claimed all space for themselves. Every single bit of land was up for grabs and could be redeemed anywhere and at any time, whether it was for the expansion of urban settlements, the extraction of raw materials, leisure and tourism, or as a cesspool or manure heap for the city. In the late modern city, there was an attempt – for technical, economic, and emotional reasons – to restore separation between cities and their surroundings.

I believe that beyond-the-modern urban design philosophy demands an entirely different approach. City and landscape are, at the very least, equal partners. Strategies guiding the transformation and development of cities should no longer be dominated by the city but can instead become interactive processes between the city and its surrounding landscape.

It is important to acknowledge that landscape, much like cities, cannot simply be reduced to a broad generalized term. With every new era and location, a city's surroundings become drastically altered. They are characterized by the confrontation with, and exposure to, the nearby city and layered with the deposits of many bygone eras. To achieve a new awareness of the unity between cities and their surroundings, we must acknowledge the individuality, complexity, and contradictions of these outer landscapes.

THE AUTONOMY OF THE LANDSCAPE

I wish to illustrate the autonomy of landscape by describing a project initiated by myself and Heinz Schöttli, city architect for the Swiss city of Zug. Through a cooperative process, we had agreed to find new options for the plain surrounding the river Lorze, a scarred landscape with many marks left by previous interventions. Based on historic interpretations of city rights, an "in-between city" (*Zwischenstadt* [121]) had developed between the autonomous cities of Zug, Cham, and Baar.

The unique landscape at the northern end of Lake Zug, to the right and left banks of the River Lorze, was increasingly encroached upon by the building and development requirements of the region's urban sprawl.

Current urban design theory describes cities as rhizomes, a system of underground links that surfaces from place to place. [122] The individual parts of this rhizome appear autonomous, but are in fact part of a greater organism. This tangle of parts was transforming the ecological and emotional significance of the Lorze plain into an urban backyard.

It seemed important to give the Lorze plain its own sense of autonomy and identity, rather than simply reducing it to a recreation area or divisive strip between the cities of Zug, Cham, and Baar. To attain this goal, we formed a cooperative called Lorze City and tried to carefully integrate this new institution into the local political system. In the project's first stage, we used workshops with three planning teams to develop a concept. The group led by landscape architect and urban planner Michael Koch, created an engaging concept based on the area's geological and biotopic structure. The project's goals were presented and discussed at public meetings involving the authorities from the concerned communities, the non-governmental organizations interested in the project, and the media. This gave local residents the opportunity to become familiar with the idea. During a second phase, the project's goals were incorporated into the regional planning concept through political resolutions. This sort of process does not instantly incite radical change in a society's attitudes toward its environment. Still, many times the only possibility for altering mindsets is to repeatedly prod gently in a certain direction.

The edge of the landscape and the edge of the city: the Lorze plain near Zug, Switzerland

Concept for integrating landscape and city

BUILDING WITH THE LANDSCAPE

The Dutch government anticipates it will
need one hundred thousand new housing
units annually throughout the next ten years.
To this end, the Dutch Ministry for Regional
Planning has adopted the Vinex Program
(Vierde Nota Extra), a strategy for identifying
potential expansion sites within existing
urban structures. Kees Christiaanse, one of
the commissioned planners for the Driel-Oost
project, writes that the point is, "not to replace
cows with houses," or landscape with city, but
to create a new symbiotic relationship with the
surrounding landscape. This approach follows
methods established by Frank Lloyd Wright's
vision for Broadacre City, Holland's Office
for Metropolitan Architecture's (OMA) design
for Melun-Sénart in France, and Dutch architect Willem Jan Neuteling's carpet metropolis.

Model of Driel-Oost, the Netherlands. "The existing structure
of lots, ditches, streets, buildings, dikes, and trees is preserved.
Not out of nostalgia, but because this structure is usable."

Elaborating on the subject, Christiaanse
writes that "One should avoid that the new
urban quarter displays the deficiencies,
which mark nearly all urban expansions of
the post-war period in the Netherlands: lack
of identity, lack of context, monofunctionality,
lack of urbanity or landscape ... The existing structure of lots, ditches, streets, buildings, dikes, and trees is preserved. Not out
of nostalgia, but because this structure is
usable ... The lots are developed or not developed. There are no large areas of continuously developed lots; they are developed in an
alternating pattern. This ensures that green
corridors and open landscape spaces remain
between the built areas. The undeveloped
lots may be existing orchards, forested areas
or meadows, but they can also accommodate
new uses such as playgrounds and playing
fields." [123]

The tetrahedron at Bottrop, designed by German architect
Wolfgang Christ

CONSECRATING THE LANDSCAPE

Thus, consecrating the landscape so to speak, means drawing attention to its presence and autonomy. This autonomy of landscape, of nature, exists a priori. We get to know it as we feel and experience its beauty. I am reminded here of the ecstatic accounts from the first astronauts who saw planet earth from the perspective of outer space. But there are also very small, brief and emotional encounters, the everyday type that may take us by surprise upon walking in the forest, sailing on a lake, or even strolling through the city.

Modern thought, with its purely physical orientation, negates this autonomy of nature. Just like the person who insists on standing alone in the world, pretending not to have parents, and refusing to acknowledge his role as part of a greater family. For several decades, a wide variety of disciplines have been devoted to helping humankind become once again conscious of the strength and energy of landscape.

Still, discussing the autonomy of landscape may lead us down the wrong path. The landscape that surrounds cities predates them and, to this day, still forms the primordial foundation of our experience. With the Western focus on the mental dimension, the self and the city become the primary forces. If we begin, however, to see ourselves as part of a greater whole, then cities too become part of a greater whole. The recent re-emergence and popularity of the term cityscape indicates that a new holistic view of the world is growing within urbanism. French landscape architect Christophe Girot eloquently described this shift.

"The semantic change of the terms 'landscape' and 'city' is so significant that we can speak of a paradigm shift ... If we accept the new paradigm of the urban landscape, then we must begin to explain urbanity in completely new terms: instead of standing in contrast to one another, landscape and city should form an alliance and complete each other. Both parts are intertwined to such a degree that they cannot exist independently of one another. New theories are formed, dealing exclusively with the landscape of the city or the architecture of the landscape ... Our cities must break with the latent pastoral archetypes that plague most developments of urban landscapes on the periphery of cities. We must develop a vocabulary for landscape architecture that is appropriate to the harsh urban reality in which we live. Urbanism will only experience a renaissance if architecture, landscape architecture, and engineering work hand in hand to improve degraded urban spaces ... Synergies as well as dialogues, expressed in a noticeable convergence of interests, must evolve between these disciplines. Today, we understand the urban environment as a complex hodge-podge of systems and superpositions of the present and the past. But it is precisely the congruence in the composition of this collected material, which must be examined and explained ... Time and its various forms of representation are ... the very key to designing all enduring landscape structures in the city ... I advocate the vision of a lasting landscape of the city, capable of better satisfying the human needs for comfort, identity, stability, and dignity." [124]

LAND ART

> The true artist helps the world by
> revealing mystic truths.
>
> *Bruce Naumann*

In the 1960s and 1970s, a new form of artistic
expression called land art evolved in the
United States. By implementing subtle changes
and interventions in a particular landscape,
land art brought the power of nature and
landscape to the attention of mindful observers. In Europe, Joseph Beuys' 7000 Oaks
project drew much attention at Documenta,
the 1982 art exhibit in the German city
of Kassel.

Works such as this indicated a new mindfulness toward land and its aesthetics. In the
1990s, the International Building Exhibition
at Emscher Park created a multitude of economic, social, and cultural initiatives to help
Germany's Ruhr region transition out of its
industrial past. As part of this project,
a lookout was created on top of a coalmine
slagheap. The climb up into the pyramid is
a breathtaking journey along a stairway construction that seemed to adhere to nothing.
At the top, one feels as though one were
soaring above the earth in a spaceship. These
works underscore a new mindfulness toward
land and its aesthetics. They are also an
important contribution toward activating
our non-rational consciousness.

On March 16, 1962, Joseph Beuys planted the first tree
for the Documenta 7 in Kassel, Germany.

Lightning Field, Walter de Maria, Quemado, New Mexico, 1977

Old Wood, Scotland, Richard Long, 1979

GEOMANCY, REINHABITATION, DEEP ECOLOGY

Geomancy taps into the subtle energies of the earth that cannot be recorded and assessed with the tools of applied science. It deals with dimensions of the earth and of its landscape that have hardly ever been explored. The word geomancy, writes geomancer Marko Pogacnik, actually means "divination – divining or telling the truth – about the hidden forces in the earth, or divination with the help of these forces." [125] As a result of the consensus among the sciences to restrict truth to that which can be scientifically proven, we have lost our sensitivity to many of the world's subtle energies. In fact, we have largely lost our ability to perceive that which is not material.

When birds return to the same nesting place as the previous year after migrating thousands of kilometers, they are probably following these energies. When people are able to locate water underground with the help of divining rods, they are sensing signals that occur outside of the scientific spectrum. My friend Ruedi Schmid taught me how to read people's auras. He sees auras in different colors and is able to gather vast amounts of detailed information about people by reading them. I see auras only as a bright sphere of light surrounding the person I am looking at. I remain at a kindergarten level of proficiency in this particular discipline. No doubt, there are tremendous untapped potentials available to us in this area. Unconsciously, however, we all continuously feel, sense, and intuit information about other people, or nature, that is not scientifically quantifiable.

In Schule der Geomantie (School of Geomancy), Pogacnik counts urban design and architecture among those areas "through which man can make a creative contribution to the fullness of the existing geomantic phenomena in a natural space. A city, for example, or a building, represent richly structured geomantic force fields in themselves. Set into the geomantic systems of the landscape, they provoke a vital interaction and certain transformational processes. Aquastates and other, secondary-force phenomena of the structure-giving dimension are the resulting traces of this interaction. The transformations that are set in motion create new force linkages and lead to mutations and further developments in the domain of the vital element organs of the landscape.

Unfortunately, this constructive aspect has a dark side as well. When architects and urban designers do not pay sufficient attention to their intuitive instincts and have no training or knowledge of geomancy, they may make grave errors, which damage the site or landscape's geomantic organism and instill unhealthy vibrations in the buildings or entire urban districts. The aim of incorporating the study of geomancy in the general curricula for urban planning, architecture, and design would be to avoid the undesired dark sides when culture and nature meet and to promote the constructive aspect [of this interaction]." [126]

The deep ecology movement is closest in spirit to the original Taoist philosophy of feng shui. As early as 1972, author Arne Naess drew attention to the difference between "a superficial, but currently fairly strong movement" and "a deep, but currently less influential movement." He defined the superficial movement as a "fight against environmental pollution and wasteful use of resources. The focus is on the health of the individual in developed countries." Conversely, a "rejection of the idea of man in the environment in favor of the idea of configuration of relationships, of the integrated system," was his definition for the deep ecology movement. "One way to begin the re-inhabitation of a place is to set aside a tiny bit of ruined land as a nature shrine. Replant it with native vegetation, which will in turn lead to native small animals and birds returning. From this small beginning, others will soon realize the diversity of plants they have lost … Such a nature shrine will not be a park in the usual sense. It will not be for recreation in the usual mindless sense but for the 're-creation' both of ourselves and the natural environment."[127] We may begin with an even simpler step: creating propitious conditions to make this re-creation possible in the first place.

"At the age of eighty, the scholar-diplomat and painter Wen Zhenming (1470–1559) painted an old, gnarled cypress and a solid rock in ink on paper, giving these ancient symbols of continuity a new interpretation. He composed a small poem, inscribed on the upper left corner: 'Weighed down by snow, attacked by frost, her branches are twisted in the course of months and years and her crown is bent, and yet her strength remains majestic'."
(Ebrey, Patricia Buckley; China, Campus, Frankfurt, p.199)

Town planner Cornelis Von Esteren (1897–1988)
attempting to achieve an overview

———

AS IT IS SAID THAT THE TAO AS DESCRIBED IS NOT THE REAL TAO,
SO ONE MIGHT SAY THAT TE (VIRTUE OR VIRTUALITY) AS EITHER
CONTRIVED OR PRESCRIBED IS NOT GENUINE TE.

— *Alan Watts* [128]

PREMISE:
IF THE AFOREMENTIONED FIVE
CONCEPTS ARE TAKEN SERIOUSLY,
THE CULTURE AND POLITICS OF
URBANISM WILL BECOME ENRICHED
AND THE URBANIST'S PROFESSION
AS A WHOLE WILL BECOME INFUSED
WITH FRESH ENERGY AND NEW
CHALLENGES.

Te refers to how we deal with the world based on our sense of what Alan Watts calls virtue. Therefore, I believe that one could also translate *te* to mean attitude. Attitude is a philosophy of life that is based on knowledge and awareness of things. When this attitude is determined by rigid rules and moral laws, then it becomes what Watts called "contrived or prescribed," and thus not "genuine *te*." But when it is natural, then it is genuine *te*.

As we search for a new culture and politics of urbanism in the beyond-the-modern age, we will discover a new job profile for all partners involved in the transformation of the city. It is my hope that this new *te* has revealed itself among the examples and arguments in the preceding chapters.
Rather than formulating a summary conclusion, I have instead chosen three quotes written, respectively, by an American, an Italian, and a Dutchman.

The first, by philosopher Richard Tarnas, outlines the cultural challenge we face today. A compelling interpreter of our times, Tarnas' perspective is rooted in what I view as a distinctly United States-based effort to reach beyond the traditional boundaries of modern Western philosophy.

"For the deepest passion of the Western mind has been to reunite with the ground of its being. The driving impulse of the West's masculine consciousness has been its dialectical quest not only to realize itself, to forge its own autonomy, but also, finally, to recover its connection with the whole, to come to terms with the great feminine principle in life: to differentiate itself from but then rediscover and reunite with the feminine, with the mystery of life, of nature, of soul." [129]

The second quote, by author Umberto Eco, addresses how we should meet the challenges of the beyond-the-modern era. A keen observer of our age, Eco is rooted in the curiosity of the Italian Renaissance and the skepticism of old Europe.

"Our own Middle Ages, it has been said, will be an age of 'permanent transition' for which new methods of adjustment will have to be employed. The problem will not so much be that of preserving the past scientifically as of developing hypotheses for the exploitation of disorder, entering into the logic of conflictuality ... The Middle Ages preserved in its way the heritage of the past but not through hibernation, rather through a constant retranslation and reuse; it was an immense work of bricolage, balanced among nostalgia, hope, and despair." [130]

The third quote, by Rem Koolhaas, surprisingly enough given his background, deals with the practice and professional image of the architect and urban planner. An eloquent spokesman for new urbanism, Koolhaas is rooted in the Marxist rationalism of a global-minded citizen of the world.

"What if we simply declare that there *is* no crisis – redefine our relationship with the city not as its makers but as its mere subjects, as its supporters?" [131]

Against this backdrop, laboring in urbanism could become a laboratory for the beyond-the-modern world.

APPENDIX

NØTES

1 Italo Calvino, *Invisible Cities*, trans. William Weaver
  (San Diego, New York, London: Harcourt, 1974) pp. 5, 165.
2 Eduard Renner, *Goldener Ring über Uri* (Neuchâtel:
  Mühlrad-Verlag H.R. Müller, 1954) p. 36.
3 Heinrich Schmidt (ed.), *Philosophisches Wörterbuch*
  (Stuttgart: Alfred Körner Verlag, 1982) p. 545.
4 Calvino, p. 7.
5 Calvino, p. 32.
6 Calvino, p. 105.
7 Martin Heidegger, "Building, Dwelling, Thinking," in
  Poetry, Language, Tought, trans. Albert Hofstadter (New
  York: Harper & Row, 1971) pp. 143-161. Cited in: Neil Leach,
  Rethinking Architecture (London: Routledge, 1997) p. 101.
8 The Building Gap: 137 Suggestions on How to Fill
  it a Century Later By Rudolf Schilling
  The present is not condemned to imitating history.
  The protection of historic buildings is not an inviolable
  principle and people can once again build self-confidently
  even in historical neighborhoods. In fact, new ideas are
  welcome. This is the message from the city of Basel.
  In an inspired decision, Carl Fingerhuth, three years into
  his job as state architect (after working as an architect
  and planner in Zurich), decided to fill a vacant lot in
  the old city with a new building that didn't necessarily
  need to look old. Consequently, the city's building department staged a nationwide architectural competition in
  the spring of 1981 as a "contribution to the 1981 European
  campaign for urban renewal." The interest shown throughout Switzerland in this small building project exceeded
  all expectations: 304 architects from all over the country
  requested the competition guidelines; 137 submitted
  proposals. As a result, the smallest of properties became
  the scene for a national celebration of architecture.
  The street containing the vacant lot (owned by the
  city of Basel) is called Spalenvorstadt. It is located on the
  western perimeter of the old city and runs from the so-
  called Lyss to the Spalentor. Like most of old Basel, it came
  into being shortly after the great earthquake of 1356.
  Some of the street's buildings have been altered, reconstructed, and replaced a number of times over the centuries. Although Spalenvorstadt is not a purely medieval
  construction, and therefore not listed as a first-class
  historical-preservation monument, it is nevertheless part
  of a protected zone.
  For more than a century, Spalenvorstadt 11 has remained
  empty. City archives contain only vague information
  about the structure that once occupied the lot. There are
  no old plans or elevations that would permit precise
  historical reconstruction. "The aim is to show that it is
  also possible to build in a historical ensemble using contemporary forms and materials, provided that due respect
  is shown to the cultural heritage," states the competition
  jury report. The architects were free to fill the lot as they
  pleased. Neither the use of the gap, nor the height of
  the building designed to fill it was prescribed. The only
  stipulation was that fire engines be allowed to reach the
  street from the fire station in the courtyard through
  a five-meter-wide gate.
  The jury, which included professors Paul Hofer from Bern
  and Dolf Schnebli and Ernst Studer, both from Zurich's
  Swiss Federal Institute of Technology, met in October and
  November 1981. In December, the projects were exhibited

in Basel. In February 1982, the city building department
published a report on all 137 projects.
The result? How did Swiss architects respond to the
challenge of filling a vacant lot in the old city? There are
no architectural innovations to report here, rather a
bewil dering diversity of designs. All in all, the result is a
large collection of historical references: a compendium
of architectural styles both historical (from Renaissance
to Jugendsti and Art Deco) and modern (from Groplus,
to Mies, to Wright, to Venturi). Everything seemed possible.
A few of the entries are illustrated here. I selected them
independently from the jury's decision. My intention
was to show the most important types of proposals and
to convey an idea of the broad spectrum of designs
submitted. Of the various types, I have obviously chosen
those examples that I found most convincing.
Frank Romero, an architect from Zurich, won the first
prize. In a rather traditional manner, his entry integrates
elements of Neues Bauen from the 1930s. In his project
report, Romero explicitly names Professor O. R. Salvisberg
as his inspiration. (Salvisberg's designs include the
Bleicherhof building in Bleicherweg, Zurich, 1939–1940.)
The jury's decision in favor of this cross between "historic"
and "modern" elements is cautious if not fainthearted.
[3rd column, top down:]
A gap remains a gap: The framework clearly identifies
the gap as such: "This is a hole," say the rods. The most
prominent representatives of this so-called postmodern
architectural language are Americans Venturi and Rauch.
(Project by Walter Tüscher and Michel Voillat, architects
BSA, Freiburg.)
[Kristallpalästchen:]
A miniature Crystal Palace: This glass house stands
assertively amidst the sequence of historical facades.
"I am a new building. Don't I look elegant?" it seems to
say. This entry follows the steel-and-glass architectural
tradition, most famously represented by Mies van
der Rohe. (Project by Ernst and Beth Stocker, Basel.)
[Öko-Architektur]
Eco architecture: The glass body has a double skin and
could be equipped with solar collectors – an energy-
saving house. Its external structure recalls the neo-Gothic
approach of German architect Gottfried Böhm. (Project
by Jürg B. Grunder, Ostermundigen, and Rolf von Allmen,
Bollingen.)
[4th column]
[Neoklassizismus]
Neo-classicism: The broad-shouldered façade uses
classical forms: the round arch, the square, the column,
and the frieze. It exemplifies the current tendency to
apply anew the monumental elements of Roman and
Renaissance architecture. (Project by Felix Schwarz, Rolf
Gutmann, Hans Schüpach, and Frank Gloor, Basel and
Zurich.)
[Überbrückung:]
Bridging the gap: Here, the neighboring buildings are
extended beyond the gap. Both sides are "knitted" so that
the new section merges with the old buildings. This entry
exemplifies an effort to find the best possible solution
for repairing city structures. (Project by Bernhard Hoesli,
Jürg Jansen, and Stephan Lucek, Zurich.)

[Bio-Architektur:]
Bio-architecture: The gap appears to be "overgrown," creating the impression both sides are encroaching uncontrollably upon the gap. This organic approach mildly references Frank Lloyd Wright and, perhaps, Rudolf Steiner. (Project by Florian Vischer and Georges Weber, Basel.)
[5th column]
[Dorf in der Stadt:]
A village in the city: It looks like a reconstructed barn. Rural and urban traditions are juxtaposed. In the city, as in a highway restaurant, there ought to be a slight smell of hay. Seldwyla dispels all weariness with modernism. (Project by Trix and Robert Haussmann, Zurich.)
[Urbaner Traditionalismus:]
Urban traditionalism: A posh townhouse fills the gap. The architecture playfully adopts formal elements of the neighboring houses and transforms them into a version of late Jugendstil. Although the new building is adapted to its surroundings, it wants to look grand. "Aren't I the most beautiful house on the entire street?" (Project by René Haubensak, Zurich.)
[Rekonstruktion:]
Reconstruction: This is how it might have looked. The town plan drawn in 1615 by Matthäus Merian shows two houses at this location. The vacant lot is filled in the most plausible way from a monument-protection standpoint. The result says, "There never was a vacant lot here." (Project by Heinz Forster, Frauenfeld.)
Excerpted from Tagesanzeiger-Magazin, January 16, 1982

9 Neue Zürcher Zeitung, "Aus engen Baracken in lichte Hallen," April 9, 2003, p. 39.
10 Marc Angélil, "Terminal Space," Archithese 5 '02, p. 12.
11 Angélil, p. 15.
12 Cheap and Easy: But Is That Really Enough?
    By Carl Fingerhuth
What the president of the government of the Canton of Zurich was, unfortunately, unable to say at the opening of the Fingerdock at Kloten Airport.

At the official opening of the Vienna State Opera, emperor Franz Joseph allegedly made some critical remarks about the new building. Shortly thereafter, the Opera's architect committed suicide. Subsequently, every time Franz Joseph attended the opening of a public building, he apparently restricted himself to saying: "It was very nice. I was very pleased."

When the new Fingerdock at Kloten Airport opened last autumn, the official speeches praised the building's timely completion and how easy it was to care for. Not a word was mentioned about the architecture. Were people afraid that the architect might kill himself?

It is said that every nation gets the government it deserves. It probably gets the architecture it deserves too. The buildings of any age always reflect the prevailing social, economic, and cultural conditions. During the early Middle Ages, the people of Zurich erected the Grossmünster church to the glory of God. Later, Zurich's middle classes documented its claims to power by building a prestigious town hall. Before World War II, young architects Haefeli, Moser, and Steiger won a competition to design the city's convention center. They demonstrated

their open-mindedness and faith in the future of the town through novel architectural designs erected at a prominent location on the banks of Lake Zurich. Architecture has always been historiography.

The various construction phases of Kloten Airport also form a historical record.

In 1953, Terminal A opened to the public. The building stands in the tradition of the finest Swiss architecture from the 1930s to 1950s: Salvisberg, Hofmann, Baur. From the overall concept right down to the nitty-gritty details, the design was extremely carefully conceived. The access road, the banisters, the flooring, and the control tower all display the same high-quality concept. A spacious, bright hall with a high window opens out onto the great wide world. The building's architectural language, primarily formed out of traditional elements, conveys optimism and faith in the future, while its details reflect the considerable care taken in designing it. The quality of the whole testifies to an approach in which an overall concept was combined with attention to detail. Terminal A was clearly meant to be a totally Swiss structure.

Its origins are rooted in a tradition of high architectural culture and the government's commitment to that culture. Characteristic of the time in which it was constructed, nobody apparently gave any thought to a possible extension. Political consciousness had not yet discovered exponential growth curves. And people believed that when the building was finished, the airport problem would be solved once and for all.

In the late 1960s, when the next planning phase began, the situation had altered dramatically. This time there were no limits to growth, the public sector was prospering, and internationalism had gained wide currency. Indeed, terminal B became an international architectural machine. There were neither emotional gestures nor vistas of the great wide world, but there was proficient design, and everything was organized to ensure the highest degree of perfection. It was indistinguishable from any other new international airports in Africa or America.

In 1975, further extension became necessary. The concerns of 1953 had ceased to interest people, and by this time, the serial design quality of 1975 had become a golden calf. In 1985, the Fingerdock opened. Construction cost three hundred million Swiss Francs. During peak periods, it has the energy consumption of a town of ten thousand inhabitants. Every hour, thirty five thousand cubic meters of fresh air have to be processed. From the outside, one sees a floating concrete box with a control tower that resembles a cheap coffeemaker. Inside, the building has the atmosphere of a warehouse, and lacks both ambience and any relationship to its function or location.

In his speech at the Fingerdock's inauguration, the president of Zurich's government never alluded to the building's architectural quality. This was clearly not, his speech seemed to imply, another contribution by the public sector to Switzerland's rich architectural culture. Had it been so, he might have said: "Following the tradition of the station buildings constructed around the turn of the last century, the postal service buildings erected in the past few years around Zurich and Lucerne, and the

national expressway tunnels in Ticino, governmental authorities have tried to create a work that fulfils their cultural obligations. It is intended to document our commitment to designing the environment in a way that makes it human, with designs that consider the emotional needs of human beings. This work is intended to show that culturally responsible architecture goes beyond mere function and solidity. And, above all, that a building must leave its mark on the outside world. Travelers from all over the globe should be able to see that we are not solely interested in designing a world based on deadlines, cost-effectiveness and ease of care."
It is a shame that this speech could not be delivered. One consolation, however, is the certain knowledge that when the time comes for the Fingerdock to be demolished, the Zurich landmark protection agency is unlikely to submit an application for it to be listed as worthy of protection.

13 Klaus Humpert (ed.), *Stadterweiterung: Freiburg Reiselfeld* (Stuttgart: avedition, 1977) p. 29.

14 Jean Gebser, *The Ever-Present Origin*, trans. Noel Barstad with Algis Mickunas (Ohio: Ohio University Press, 1986) p. 1.

15 Gebser, p. 36.

16 Gebser, p. 117.

17 "Montezuma's Castle" in Arizona, USA, erected by the Sinagua Indians circa 1100.

18 René Descartes, *Discourse on Method and Meditations on First Philosophy*, trans. Donald A. Cress (Indianapolis: Hackett, 1998) p. 7.

19 Rupert Sheldrake, *The Rebirth of Nature* (London: Random, 1990) p. xiv.

20 Sheldrake, p. 81.

21 Victor Hugo, *Notre-Dame of Paris*, trans. John Sturrock, (London: Penguin, 1978) p. 129. Cited in: Vittorio Magnano Lampugnani, *Architektur als Kultur* (Cologne, 1986) p. 17.

22 Hermann Bortfeldt, *Die französische Revolution* (Munich: Heyne, 1989) p. 129.

23 Le Corbusier, *Towards a New Architecture*, trans. John Rodker, in: *Essential Le Corbusier L'Esprit Nouveau Articles* (Oxford: Architectural Press, 1998) p. 25.

24 Ken Wilber, *The Marriage of Sense and Soul – Integrating Science and Religion* (New York: Random House, 1998) pp. 12, 13.

25 Wilber, pp. 119ff.

26 Gregory Bateson, *Steps to an Ecology of the Mind* (San Francisco: Chandler, 1972) p. 500.

27 Le Corbusier, *The City of To-morrow and Its Planning*, trans. John Rodker, in: *Essential Le Corbusier L'Esprit Nouveau Articles* (Oxford: Architectural Press, 1998) p. 5.

28 Benedikt Huber and Christian Süsstrunk (eds.), *Die Bedeutung der Form* (Zurich: Verlag der Fachvereine, 1988) p. 7.

29 Werner Durth and Niels Gutschow, *Träume in Trümmern* (Munich: dtv, 1993), pp. 137ff.

30 André Bideau, "Ende der Avantgarde," *werk, bauen + wohnen*, 10/2001, p. 8.

31 HRH The Prince of Wales, *A Vision of Britain* (London: Doubleday, 1989) p. 123.

32 C. G. Jung, *Answer to Job*, trans. R. F. C. Hull (London: Routledge & Kegan Paul, 1954) pp. 52, 53.

33 Venturi / Scott Brown / Izenour, *Learning from Las Vegas* (Cambridge: MIT Press, 1972) p. 72.

34 Hans Küng, *Global Responsibility* (New York: Crossroad, 1991) p. 21.

35 Richard Wilhelm, [trans. into German] and C. G. Jung [commentary], *The Secret of the Golden Flower* (A Chinese Book of Life), trans. Cary F. Baynes (London, 1931) pp. 81, 82.

36 Marita Beck, in *Der Architekt* 5/98, p. 275.

37 Theodor W. Adorno, *Aesthetic Theory*, trans. Robert Hullot-Kentor (Minneapolis: University of Minnesota Press, 1997) p. 23.

38 Venturi / Scott / Brown / Izenour

39 Alan Watts, *The Watercourse Way* (New York: Pantheon Books, 1975)

40 Carl Fingerhuth and Ernst Joos (eds.), *The Kunming Project* (Basel: Birkhäuser, 2002).

41 Venturi / Scott / Brown / Izenour, p. 8.

42 Robert Venturi, *Complexity and Contradiction in Architecture* (New York: MoMA, 1977) p. 16.

43 Le Corbusier, *Towards a New Architecture*, trans. John Rodker, in: *Essential Le Corbusier L'Esprit Nouveau Articles* (Oxford: Architectural Press, 1998) pp. 29, 131.

44 Giuliano Gresleri, *Le Corbusier, Viaggio in Oriente*, (Venice, 1984) p. 305.

45 Hassan Fathy, cited in: Georg Gerster, *Nubien* (Zurich: Artemis, 1964) p.185.

46 Hassan Fathy, *Architecture for the Poor* (Chicago: The University of Chicago Press, 1976).

47 Heinrich Klotz, afterword to the German edition of Venturi, pp.217ff.

48 Watts, pp. 41, 42ff.

49 François Jullien, *Detour and Access: Strategies of Meaning in China and Greece* (New York: Zone Books, 2000) p. xx.

50 Roman Malek, *Das Tao des Himmels* (Freiburg: Herder, 1996) p. 24.

51 Joseph Needham, in: Colin A. Ronan, *The Shorter Science and Civilisation in China – An Abridgement of Joseph Needham's Original Text*, Vol. 1, (London: Cambridge University Press, 1978) p. 166.

52 A. Reichwein, *China und Europa* (Berlin, 1923) p.89.

53 Needham, p. 247.

54 Wilhelm / Jung, p. 3.

55 Wilhelm / Jung, pp. 25ff.

56 Wilhelm / Jung, pp. 94/95.

57 Wilhelm / Jung, p. 94.

58 Wilhelm / Jung, pp. 136/137.

59 Watts, p. XV.

60 Watts, p. 37.

61 Philip Ursprung (ed.), Herzog & de Meuron: *Natural History* (Montréal: Canadian Centre for Architecture and Lars Müller Publishers, 2002) p. 111.

62 Dorothee Huber, *Architekturführer Basel* (Basel: Architekturmuseum Basel, 1993) p. 407.

63 Friedrich Nietzsche, *The Birth of Tragedy*, trans. Shaun Whiteside (London: Penguin, 1993) p. 98.

64 Hilar Stadler, "Malerei-Wand-Malerei von Peter Roesch," in: Patrick Gmür, *Eine Kinderstadt, Erweiterung Schulanlage Scherr* (Lucerne: Quart, 2003) p. 45.

65 Adolf Max Vogt, *Neue Zürcher Zeitung*, February 11, 2003, p. 26.

66 DB mobil, customer magazine, 2003.

67 Kenneth Frampton, "Towards a Critical Regionalism,"
in: Hal Foster (ed.), The Anti-Aesthetic – Essays on Postmodern Culture (Seattle: Bay Press, 1983) p. 29.

68 Tages-Anzeiger, Zurich, September 10, 2003, p. 10.

69 Pascal Amphoux, "Aux écoutes de la ville," Report 10
of the National Research Program "City and Traffic,"
Schweizerischer Nationalfonds (Berne, 1994).

70 Ken Wilber, No Boundary: Eastern and Western
Approaches to Personal Growth (Boston: Shambala
Publishing, 2001).

71 Pierre Teilhard de Chardin, Die Entstehung des Menschen
(Munich: Beck, 1961).

72 Sheldrake.

73 Stanislav Grof, Geburt, Tod und Transzendenz
(Kösel, 1985).

74 Watts, p. 3.

75 SonntagsZeitung, Zurich, September 1st, 2002.

76 Gottfried Semper, Kleine Schriften (reprint, Mittenwald,
1979) p. 351.

77 Wolfgang Welsch, Ästhetisches Denken (Stuttgart:
Reclam, 1991) p. 11.

78 Alfred Schinz, The Magic Square, Cities in Ancient China
(Stuttgart / London: Axel Menges) p. 416.

79 Nelson Wu, Chinese and Indian Architecture
(new York: George Braziller, 1963) p. 46.

80 Michael Egloff, "werk, bauen und wohnen," 05/2001, p. 61.

81 Seyfert, Werner; Walddorfschule in D-Heidenheim
(unpublished manuscript, 1974) p. 3.

82 Watts, pp. 19, 20.

83 Aldous Huxley, The Perennial Philosophy (London: Chatto
& Windus, 1972) p. 16.

84 Stefano Bianca, Urban Form in the Arab World
(New York: Thames and Hudson, 2000) p. 342.

85 Jack Kornfield, Frag den Buddha und geh den Weg
des Herzens (Munich: Econ, 2001) p. 63.

86 Alfred Schinz, Cities in China (Berlin, Stuttgart, 1989)
pp. 291ff.

87 Marco Polo, The Travels, trans. Ronald Latham
(London: Penguin, 1958) pp. 177ff.

88 Watts, p. 75.

89 Watts

90 John Blofeld, Taoism – The Quest for Immortality
(London: Mandala Books, 1979) p. 10.

91 Tao Te Ching, verse 60.

92 Wolfgang Welsch, Vernunft (Frankfurt: Suhrkamp, 1995)
p. 796.

93 Kevin Kelly, Out of Control (Boulder: Perseus Publishing,
1995) p. 5.

94 Arif Hasan, Community Initiatives (Karachi: City Press,
1998) p. 83.

95 In the spiritual theory, which was also adopted by
Rudolf Steiner, it would be 42 and not 40 years: that is,
6 x 7 years or 3 x 14 years. I began my independent
professional career at the age of 28, assumed the office
of city architect at age 42, and resigned from the
position at age 52.

96 Department of Building and Development, Zurich:
Quartier Leutschenbach (Zurich, 1999) pp. 7, 28.

97 Department of Building and Development, Zurich, p. 28.

98 Sichtung 1, Bilanz zur Qualifikation von Planen
und Bauen in Feldkirch 1997-99, Stadt Feldkirch, 2000.

99 Suddenly, However, Everything Changed
Carl Fingerhuth on the Malicious Seduction of Naïve
Adults

I was also a naïve adult. As a member of Salzburg's
urban design advisory board for four years, I experienced
responsible cultural policies aimed at promoting high-
quality architecture and urban design. We had a dedicated
city council that listened to us and shared responsibility
for challenging decisions, an administration that consis-
tently demanded precisely worded statements, and a
public accustomed to openness. Naïve and full of trust
as I was, I accepted being elected to a jury created by the
state, rather than the city, of Salzburg. It was our job
to assist the Salzburg Festival's board of trustees in its
search for a design for a new festival hall.
Five architects from three different countries were
selected. On very short notice, they were asked to design
projects for an incredibly ambitious task. The projects were
presented to the jury, which decided in favor of a project
co-designed by Luxemburg firm Hermann & Valentiny
and Salzburg firm Wimmer Zaic.
Suddenly, however, everything changed. What would
follow was, to a naïve person like myself, an unbelievable
and incomprehensible series of political machinations
and manipulations.
The honorable architect Wilhelm Holzbauer, whose
design had only placed second, lodged an objection with
the Federal Procurement Office concerning the winning
project. It was evident that he had access to detailed
information about the winning project that could have
only been given to him by the state of Salzburg.
An application was filed by the representative for the
state prime minister stating that since the winning
project contained violations, the honorable architect who
had placed second ought to be commissioned to implement the project, even though his project also contained
a number of serious violations.
When this move proved fruitless, the order was given
for the entries to be judged again. To make sure that this
would be to the advantage of the honorable architect,
the ground rules were changed. This time around, the
architects invited to submit entries were encouraged to
form teams amongst themselves. Massive pressure was
applied on the winning architects from the first round to
team up with the honorable architect. In this connection,
architect Francy Valentiny told me that, among other
forms of pressure, he had received a phone call from his
native country of Luxembourg's foreign minister.
During the preliminary project examination by the state
administration, there was no mention of the fact that
the honorable architect had failed to observe the fire reg-
ulations. To have done so would have meant a considerable reduction in the number of seats in the festival hall,
and thus led to the rejection of a project praised for its
economic efficiency.
To be on the safe side, a majority vote by the jury
eliminated Robert Wimmer's project during the second
judgment round based on formal grounds: he had
refused to play the merger game, preferring to submit
his own project.
Unfortunately, however, the jury's new judgment did not
produce the expected "correct" result. A clear majority

had now voted in favor of the project by Swiss firm Bétrix & Consolascio. Consequently, for the sixth time, the old box of tricks was dragged out again. The jury's decision was overturned by a report submitted by a civil engineer, thus placing the honorable architect first. No civil engineer was represented on the jury. Instead there were theatre experts, state and city representatives, a committee of city preservation experts, members of the Salzburg Festival's board of trustees, as well as independent and neutral advisers.

The entire procedure contained a number of grave offences, which leave me feeling very uneasy:

A democratically legitimated state government stages a sham competition. Two times over, four architects invest several thousand euro even though, from the very beginning, the state government intends to commission only its honorable friend to do the job. In my understanding of the law, this is malicious deception.

To attain this end, the state government follows procedures established in Europe specifically to prevent mafia-style practices for awarding contracts. In so doing, it discredits the battle against corruption between politicians and business people and lays itself wide open to the very same accusation.

The practice of choosing architectural and urban-design projects through competitive procedures is one of the most important instruments for creating social, economic, and cultural quality within towns. It is also the most important instrument for giving young architects an opportunity to make a name for themselves against an aging, sometimes even corrupt, establishment. It was this procedure that led to the Rialto in Venice (several centuries ago), the Centre Pompidou in Paris, and the new Tate Gallery in London. Thus considered, the selection process for the Salzburg festival hall is a cultural catastrophe.

I should like to close with a personal comment. After the participants and the jury had been discredited a second time, I was actually expecting this decision to trigger a public discussion in Salzburg and Austria. Being a foreigner to that city and country, I did not think that it would be right for me to comment on their political and cultural situation. Nevertheless, I have chosen to write this article because I feel that many of my Austrian friends were not even aware that such shocking things were happening.

100 National Geographic Magazine.

101 *Neue Zürcher Zeitung*, October 5/6, 2002.

102 Ernest J. Eitel, *Feng-Shui: The Rudiments of Natural Science in China* (Hong Kong, 1873) p. 65.

103 Eitel, p. 3.

104 Eitel, p. 83.

105 Jutta Schwarz, "Nachhaltige Entwicklung," *Schweizer Ingenieur und Architekt*, No. 8, February 20, 1997, p. 10.

106 Gernot Böhme, *Aisthetik* (Munich: Wilhelm Fink, 2001) p. 23.

107 Eitel, p. 6.

108 Marko Pogacnik, *Die Schule der Geomantie* (Munich: Knaur, 1996) p. 9.

109 Hans Küng and Julia Ching, *Chinesische Religion* (Munich/Zurich: Piper, 1999) p. 13.

110 Malek, pp. 41ff.

111 Blofeld, pp. 7ff.

112 Needham, p. 198.

113 Malek, p. 42.

114 Carlos Castaneda, *The Teachings of Don Juan* (Berkeley: University of California Press, 1969) pp. 16 ff.

115 Rolf d'Aujourdhui, "Das Belchen-Dreieck," *Die Wochenzeitung für das Dreiland*, June 18, 1992, pp. 3ff.

116 Robert Bauval and Graham Hancock, *Keeper of Genesis* (London: Heinemann, 1996) pp. 36, 81, 303.

117 Spiro Kostof, *The City Shaped – Urban Patterns and Meanings through History* (London: Thames and Hudson, 1991) p. 24, Pl. 7.

118 The First Scofield Reference Bible; OUP and Scofield, 1986, *Revelation*, 21: 12-14, p. 1352.

119 Titus Burckhardt, *Mirror of the Intellect, Essays on Traditional Science & Sacred Art*, trans. William Stoddart (Albany: State University of New York Press, 1987) pp. 102, 103.

120 Peter Herrle, *Vom Mandala zum Flächennutzungsplan* [dissertation Universität Stuttgart, 1983, p. 72] cited in: *Alfred Ribi, Zentrizität in der Stadtarchitektur – Verlust der Mitte*, unpublished manuscript, p. 10.

121 Thomas Sieverts, *Zwischenstadt*, 3rd edition, Bauwelt Fundamente 118, Wiesbaden 1999.

122 Dieter Geissbühler, Michael Koch, Stefan Rotzler, *Grüne Mitte Lorzenstadt* (Niggli, Sulgen/Zurich: archithese, 2000) pp. 28ff.

123 Kees Christiaanse and Angela Mensing (eds.), *Suburbia in Holland* (Berlin: Technische Universität Berlin, 1997) p. 15.

124 Christophe Girot, "Zukünftige Landschaft," *werk, bauen und wohnen*, 5/2003, pp. 48ff.

125 Pogacnik, p. 9.

126 Pogacnik, pp. 499ff.

127 Dolores LaChapelle, *Earth Wisdom* (Los Angeles: The Guild of Tutors Press, 1978) p.133.

128 Watts, p. 106.

129 Richard Tarnas, *The Passion of the Western Mind – Understanding the Ideas That Have Shaped Our World View* (New York: Ballantine, 1991) p. 443.

130 Umberto Eco "The Return of the Middle Ages," in: *Travels in Hyperreality*, trans. William Weaver (Orlando: Harcourt, Brace, Jovanovich, 1986) p. 84.

131 Rem Koolhaas and Bruce Mau, *S,M,L,XL* (New York: The Monacelli Press, 1995) p. 971.

SQUATTER SETTLEMENT IN THE DESERT ON THE OUTSKIRTS OF CHIMBOTE, PERU

Until the beginning of the twentieth century, Chimbote was a quiet fishing village, a popular honeymoon destination ... Aside from Lima ... the development [of Chimbote] is Peru's most spectacular example of urban growth ... making it Peru's fifth largest city, even though nearly every building was destroyed in the earthquake of 1970.

2003 by Hotels 4 Travellers

LA VALLETTA, MALTA

Valletta was to become "Europe's shield," an impenetrable bulwark against the Turks in the Mediterranean. The Pope dispatched Francesco Laparelli to Malta; ... he had been Michelangelo's right-hand man during the construction of St Peter's Dome ... (What emerged was) the first 'drawing-board' city of modern times based on the old Roman chessboard pattern ... His successors set the representational buildings harmoniously into this grid: the monastery church, the palace of the Grand Master (of the Order of St. John of Jerusalem), the manors of the knights ... in addition to military hospitals, hospitals and other houses of worship ... In their report, the International Council of Monuments and Sites (ICOMOS) expressed no difficulty in accepting the candidacy of Valetta (as a world heritage site). No other city of comparable compactness and density created in the late Renaissance has been preserved with so few changes: 320 historic buildings occupy an area of only 55 hectares ... The world heritage designation was awarded after the application in 1980.

Gerster, Georg; Neue Zürcher Zeitung, February 18, 1999

LOS ANGELES, USA

The linkages that exist between traffic concept and urban development are illustrated in the example of Los Angeles ... 50 percent of the area is utilized for traffic and parking – thus cars are given the same amount of space as all human activities combined.

The inefficient but environmentally friendly public transportation (system) was overruled in the free play of forces as a result of the urban plan and has been relegated to the background. The expansion of the expensive rapid transit network, operated by the Metropolitan Transportation Association since 1980, has been halted; despite its efficiency, the bus system, predominantly utilized by the low-income, non-white population, receives no political support from lobbyists and must make do with the oldest fleet of buses in the United States.

Adam, Hubertus; "Energieverbrauch endlos," Neue Zürcher Zeitung, April 18, 2001

ARLES, FRANCE

The medieval city, built into the amphitheatre of Arles

Benevolo, Leonardo; Die Geschichte der Stadt, Camus, Frankfurt, 1982, p. 331

SUN CITY NEAR PHOENIX, ARIZONA, USA

The Webb Development Company has been building its sun cities, since the success of the first near Phoenix, exclusively for the retired. No babies are born in these town; at least one member of the family has to be fifty, and children still at school are only tolerated as visitors. These settlements for older people are built, in flagrant violation of the prevailing opinion that old people abhor ghettos for the aged, and they are growing with youthful abandon despite (or perhaps because of) this geriatric heresy. Sun City near Phoenix has more than 52,000 inhabitants. When its architects selected the circle as the basic pattern of the town, cosmic symbolism was far from their thoughts. The curved streets serve to slow down the residential traffic and, more important still, the golf courses surrounding the city, can easily be reached on foot by every "sun citizen."

Gerster, Georg; Grand Design, the earth from above, Weidenfeld and Nicolson, London, 1988,
Figure 61, caption pp. 105, 106

OASIS TOWN OF EL OUED, ALGERIA

The capital of the Souf in the Algerian Sahara, it is a showpiece of "architecture without an architect" – the dream of every town planner ... Vaults and domes covering all living and service rooms shed the windblown sand, which settles as a sound-dampening layer on the streets. The house with courtyard is the unit of the town, which grows on the building-block system without any waste of land. ... Water rising by capillarity evaporates before it reaches the surface, and the salts dissolved in it are thereby precipitated. Thus in one zone are formed banks of almost pure gypsum, which, when roasted, can be used as mortar and for making bricks in molds. In another zone the gypsum becomes encrusted with quartz sand to form sand roses and later lus, the local name for a hard, durable brick which sets extremely well with the gypsum mortar. This explains the brick construction of the Souf houses, which is very unusual for the Sahara.

Gerster, Georg; Grand Design, the earth from above, Weidenfeld and Nicolson, London, 1988,
Figure 34, caption p. 67

HAMADAN, IRAN

Hamadan – Hagmatana in ancient Persia, and Ecbatana in Greek – was founded in the eighth century BC. It became the first capital of Medes and later the Achaemenian summer residence. Ibn Abu Sina, Avicenna, the most famous physician and scientist of his time, taught in Hamadan and died there in the eleventh century.

As described by Herodotus, the city consisted of seven concentric circles; but documented archaeological findings contradict the "father of history." Modern Hamadan, on the other hand, which was redesigned under Shah Riza Pahlavi, refers to the supposed historic circular form.

NANCY, FRANCE

The drawing below shows ... the shaft of space set into motion by the central bay of Héré's city hall as it acts as a unifying force in the composition. Across Place Royale it is precisely contained by the walls of the low facing buildings in front of the Arch of Triumph. In Place de la Carrière it is defined by the inner planes of the carefully clipped rows of trees and finally it passes through the central bay of the Government Palace into the garden behind.

Bacon, Edmund N., Design of Cities, Viking Press, 1974, p. 177

ESSAOUIRA, MOROCCO

With its completely preserved medina, exposed location on a small peninsula in a wide bay on the Atlantic coast, its picturesque fishing harbour and long sandy beach, Essaouira, formerly Mogador, is one of the most attractive cities in southern Morocco ... Essaouira is an important arts and crafts centre, known above all for its inlay work (>dominoes!) ... The city proper was founded as late as 1760 ... The town plans were designed by the French architect Théodore Cornut, who was a prisoner of the sultan.

Buchholz, Hartmut; Marokko, Dumont, Cologne, pp. 229ff

TOWN AND ISLAND OF MEXCALTITÀN, MEXICO

(The city) is situated in a lagoon on the Pacific coast ... The settlement of the island dates back far into pre-colonial, pre-Spanish times. Some researchers even tend to equate Mexcaltitàn with Aztlan, the original home of the Aztecs (= "people of Aztlan") before they moved to their historical territories in the high valley of Mexico. Aztec legends about the origin and wandering of the tribe tell of an island in the middle of an inland lake, a paradise for fishermen ad hunters of waterfowl. It is a fact that the memory of moon worship, Central America's oldest cult, lives on tenaciously in this village, and that its inhabitants are still quite convinced of the mystical-mythical significance of the circular settlement plan: for them, Mexcaltitàn is the center of the universe. The cross formed by the four main streets inside the ring road that encloses the town mirrors the division of the heavens into the "world's four corners."

Gerster, Georg; Grand Design, the earth from above, Weidenfeld and Nicolson, London, 1988, Figure 63, caption p. 105

HONG KONG

Much has been written about the competition between (Hong Kong and Shanghai). It is real and will continue to exist. Far more important, however, in my estimation, is the fact that both are part of a supranational network with other global cities and derive their strength in part from their affiliation to this network. The supranational network of 30 to 40 cities constitutes the architecture of the global, networked economic system. The cities in this network are strategic sites for the revaluation of new forms of global capitals. Some of these cities have greater strategic significance than others, but the key factor is perhaps the network itself: there is no single global city, and this differentiates today's global cities from the capitals of earlier times. Hong Kong is one of the most important cities in this network, Shanghai isn't. Nevertheless, both profit from belonging to the network.

Sassen, Saskia; Instant China, 2G, nexus, issue 10, 1999

LIST OF ILLUSTRATIONS

In the sequence of first reproduction in the text:

Fischer, Richard; British Piers, Thames & Hudson, London, 1987 — Cover

Gerster, Georg; photographer, Zumikon — 6, 10, 44, 64, 79, 87, 102, 112, 142, 172, 188 (bottom), 198, 208 (top, center, bottom), 209 (top below, center, bottom), 210 (top, center top, below), 211 (top, below)

Ernst Bruno; Der Zauberspiegel des M.C. Escher, Heinz Moos, Munich, 1978 — 8, 144

Polo, Marco; Il Milione – Die Wunder der Welt, Manesse, Zurich, 1997 — 12

Fondation Beyeler, invitation to Anselm Kiefer exhibition, Basel, 2001 — 14

Carl Fingerhuth, Zurich 16 (top, bottom), 18 (top), 23 (top, bottom), 62 (top, center, bottom), 71 (top), 72 (top), 89 (bottom), 91 (bottom), 93 (right center), 95 (center), 98 (center), 106 (top), 108 (top), 110 (left top, left bottom, center), 119 (top), 120 (left top, right top), 121 (bottom), 123 (top, bottom), 130 (left top), 133 (center), 135 (left top, right top), 138 (left top, left bottom, right top, right bottom), 139 (bottom), 147 (256), 156 (top), 166 (center, bottom), 179 (center, bottom), 182 (bottom)

Basler Zeitung, November 2, 1986, Basel — 17 (top)

Gianoncelli, Matteo, Como, Edizioni New Press sas, Como, 1999 — 18 (bottom)

Editions Lif, Casablanca — 19 (bottom), 40 (right top)

Valena, Tomas; Stadt und Topographie, Ernst & Sohn, Berlin, 1990 — 21 (top, center)

Hochbau- und Planungsamt Kanton Basel-Stadt, Basel — 22 (center), 23 (center), 36 (left bottom, right bottom), 93 (left top, left bottom), 94 (top, bottom), 110 (top right), 125 (top, center, bottom), 126 (top, bottom), 127 (both top, left bottom, right bottom), 128 (center, bottom), 129 (top, center, bottom), 130 (right top, right bottom), 131 (top), 132 (center, bottom), 148 (top), 157 (top, bottom), 158 (center), 179 (top), 181 (bottom)

Tages Anzeiger, January 16, 2003, Die Baulücke, March 8, 1986, Kostengerecht und pflegeleicht, Zurich — 24, 28

Neue Zürcher Zeitung, April 2003, Aus engen Baracken in lichte Hallen, Zurich — 26

ARGE Zayetta; Dockmidfield Flughafen Zurich, ARGE Zayetta, Zurich, 2002 — 27 (top, center, bottom)

Humpert, Klaus, ed.; Stadterweiterung Freiburg Rieselfeld, avedition, Stuttgart, 1997 — 30 (top, center, bottom), 31 (top, center, bottom), 32 (top)

Town planning office, Freiburg i.B. — 32 (bottom)

Schweizerische Landestopographie, Bern — 33, 43 (center), 61, 124 (top, bottom), 132 (top)

Surveying office of the canton Basel-city, Basel — 35 (right bottom)

Ernst Niklaus Fausch, Architects, Aarau — 37 (left bottom)

Herzog & de Meuron, Architects, Basel — 37 (right top), 132, 149 (bottom)

Diener & Diener, Architects, Basel — 37 (right center)

Swiss Federal Railways, Berne — 37 (right bottom)

Gebser, Jean; Ursprung und Gegenwart, dtv, Munich, 1988 — 38

Brunner, U.V.; Der Fuß in Sage, Brauchtum und Geschichte, Orthopädische Praxis, 18th annual edition, issue 7, Medizinische Literarische Verlagsgesellschaft mbH, D-Uelzen, 1982 — 39 (top)

Marijnissen, R.H., Ruyffelaere, P.; Bosch, Mercatorfonds, B-Antwerp, 2002 — 39 (center)

Campbell, Joseph; Die Kraft der Mythen, Artemis, Zurich, 1989 — 39 (bottom)

Wilber, Ken; Halbzeit der Evolution, Scherz, Berne, 1984 — 40 (left bottom)

Impact, www.impactphotographics.com USA — 40 (right bottom)

Schinz, Alfred; The Magic Square, Edition Axel Menges, Stuttgart — 41 (top), 108 (center, bottom), 109 (top, center, bottom), 117, 176, 183 (top), 185 (top), 187 (bottom)

Knell, Heiner; Ein Menschenbild in der Antike, Der Architekt 1/93 — 41 (center)

Benevolo, Leonardo; Die Geschichte der Stadt, Campus, Frankfurt, 1982 — 41 (bottom), 51 (right bottom), 53 (top, center), 185, 207 (top top)

Morris, A.E.J.; History of Urban Form, George Godwin, London, 1972 — 42 (top)

Dreysse, D.W.; May – Siedlungen, Walther König, Cologne, 1994 — 42 (bottom)

Bauwelt; 40/41 1993, Brussels, Bertelsmann, Berlin — 43 (top)

Sheldrake, Rupert; Die Wiedergeburt der Natur, Rowohlt, Reinbeck, 1994 — 43 (bottom)

Fingerhuth, Lisina, photographer, Hong Kong — 46

Rucker, Rudy; Die Wunderwelt der vierten Dimension, Scherz, Berne, 1987 — 48 (center)

Tod, Ian and Wheeler, Michael; Utopia, Orbis, London, 1978 — 48 (bottom), 54

Vigorelli, Giancarlo; Giotto, Rizzoli, Milan, 1974 — 49 (right center)

Sobel, Dava; Galileos Tochter, Berlin, Berlin, 1999 — 49 (left center)

Specht, Rainer; Descartes, Rowohlt, Reinbeck, 1996 — 49 (right center), 50 (left bottom)

Die zweite Schöpfung; ed. by Beneke, Sabine and Ottomeyer, Hans, Deutsches Historisches Museum, Berlin, 2002 — 50 (right center)

Der Spiegel; Schöne neue Arbeitswelt, 26/1999 — 50 (right bottom)

Utopia; ed. by Schaer, Roland; Claeys, Gregory and Tower Sargent, Lyman, The New Public Library/Oxford University Press, New York/Oxford, 2000 — 51 (left center)

Bortfeldt, Hermann, Die Französische Revolution, Heyne, Munich, 1989 — 51 (left bottom)

Ochs, Haila; Hauptstadtplanungen waren schon immer optimistisch, Bauwelt 22/2001, Bertelsmann, Berlin, — 51 (right center)

Von Moos, Le Corbusier, Huber, Frauenfeld, 1968 — 52 (top)

Architekturmuseum, Hans Schmidt exhibition, invitation, Basel, 1993 — 52 (bottom)

Kostof, Spiro; Die Anatomie der Stadt, in: Neue Zürcher Zeitung, Zurich, 1993 — 53 (right bottom), 186 (top right)

Campanella, Thomas J.; Cities from the Sky, Princeton Architectural Press, New York, 2001 — 54 (right top), 55 (top)

Albert Heinrich Steiner, ed. by Werner Oechslin, gta Verlag Zurich, 2001 — 54 (right center)

Ohne Leitbild? Städtebau in Deutschland und Europa; ed. by Heidede Becker, Johann Jessen, Robert Sander, Krämer, Stuttgart, 1998 — 55 (center), 192 (top)

Kaltenbrunner, Robert, Meyer-Künzel, Monika; Jahrmarkt oder gebautes Modell?, in: Archithese 5 2000, Zurich — 55 (right bottom)

Dethier, Jean et Guiheux; la ville, Centre Pompidou, Paris, 1994 — 57 (top)

Jencks, Charles A.; The language of post-modern architecture, Rizzoli, 1977 — 58 (bottom)

Durth, Werner; Träume in Trümmern, dtv, Munich, 1993 — 59 (top, center, bottom)

Cars for Cities, Her Majesty's Stationery Office, London, 1967 — 60 (bottom)

Fröhlich, Martin and Steinmann, Martin; Imaginäres Zürich, Huber, Frauenfeld/Stuttgart, 1975 — 61 (top)

Bernoulli, Hans; Die Stadt und ihr Boden, Verlag für Architektur, Erlenbach-Zürich, 1946 — 61 (center, bottom), 186 (center)

HRH The Prince of Wales; A Vision of Britain, Doubleday, London, 1989 Küng, Hans; Theologie im Aufbruch, Piper, 1992 — 68 (top)

Wehr, Gerhard; C. G. Jung, Rowohlt, Reinbeck, 1985 — 68 (center)

Venturi, Scott Brown, Izenour, Learning from Las Vegas, Bauwelt Fundamente 53, Vieweg, Braunschweig/Wiesbaden, 1997 — 71 (bottom)

Gresleri, Giuliano; Le Corbusier, Viaggio in Oriente, Marsilio, Venice, 1984 — 73 (top)

Le Corbusier; Ausblick auf eine Architektur, Bauwelt Fundamente 2, Vieweg, Braunschweig/Wiesbaden, 1989 — 73 (bottom)

Ricke, Herbert, Fingerhuth, Carl, Habachi, Labib and Zabkar, Louis V., Excavations from Khor-Dehmit to Bêt el-Wali, University of Chicago Press, Chicago, 1967 — 74 (top)

Gerster, Georg; Nubien, Artemis, Zurich, 1964 — 74 (bottom)

Fathy, Hassan; Architecture for the Poor, University of Chicago Press, Chicago and London, 1976 — 75, 76 (top, center, bottom), 77 (top, center)

Bettels, Altmut E. I., Traditionelle Baukunst in China, Benteli, Wabern, 2002 — 80, 184 (top)

Papyrus, Denges; Sahara, Ghardaïa, postcard, 1997 — 88

Herzog & de Meuron; Natural History, ed. by Philip Ursprung, Canadian Center for Architecture and Lars Müller, Montréal and Baden, 2002 — 92

Peter Zumthor, architect, Haldenstein — 95 (top)

Zumthor, Peter; Kunst der Klarheit, in: ZEIT Punkte 6/99, ZEIT, Hamburg, 1999 — 95 (bottom)

Photoglob Zurich; EXPO.02, Arteplage Yverdon-les-Bains, Die Wolke, postcard, 2002 — 96

Loderer, Benedikt; Konkrete Skulptur: Das Prinzip Anfärben, in: SonntagsZeitung, June 22, 2003, Zurich — 97 (top)

Gmür, Patrick; Eine Kinderstadt, Erweiterung Schulanlage Scherr, Quart, Lucerne, 2003 — 97 (bottom)

Denk, Andreas and Ito, Toyo; Sichtbar machen, was unsichtbar ist, in: Der Architekt, September 1998 — 99 (top)

Hornberger, Klaus; Lichtprojekt Bahnhof Zug, unpublished manuscript, Zurich, 2002 — 146

Der Pott kocht; in: DB mobil, April 1999, Frankfurt — 147

Wilber, Ken; Wege zum Selbst, Kösel, Munich, 1986 — 100

Bauwelt; Die letzte Seite, 10, 1999, Bertelsmann, Berlin — 106 (center)

Koch, Michael; Königsstadt und Wohngebiet?, werk, bauen+wohnen, 11/1999, Zurich — 106 (bottom)

MVRDV; Rotterdam, Schweizer Ingenieur und Architekt, 32, August 6, 1998, Zurich — 110 (right bottom)

Schettler, Ulrike; Zwischen Hang und Tal, Schweizer Ingenieur und Architekt, 35, September 1st, 2000, Zurich — 111 (top)

Seyfert, Werner; Waldorfschule in Heidenheim, unpublished manuscript, 1974 — 111 (center)

Art Unlimited Amsterdam; Kyoto, Japan; postcard, 1986 — 114

Roberts-Jones, Philippe and Françoise; Pieter Breughel der Ältere, Hirmer, Munich, 1997 — 116 (top, center)

Imo State Capital Owerri; Fingerhuth and Partners, Zurich, 1977 — 118 (top, bottom), 122 (top), 156 (bottom)

Daily Star, Owerri, 1977 — 119 (center), 120 (left center)

Miloni, Reto; architect, Zurich — 119 (bottom), 121 (center)

Mack, Gerhard; Herzog & de Meuron, Birkhäuser, Basel, 1997 — 131 (bottom)

Helbling, Andrea; photographer, Zurich — 133 (top)

Architektur für Basel; ed. by Bruno Chiavi, Fritz Schumacher, Friedrich Weissheimer, Birkhäuser, Basel, 2001 — 133 (bottom)

The Kunming Project; ed. Carl Fingerhuth and Ernst Joos, Birkhäuser, Basel, 2002 — 134, 135 (left center, right bottom), 136, 139 (bottom), 140 (top, center, bottom), 141 (left top, right top, bottom), 159 (left bottom, right top, center, bottom)

Edivision, Casablanca; Place Moulay Hassan, Essaouira, postcard, 2002 — 147 (top)

Tiefbauamt Basel-Stadt, Basel, 2002 — 148 (center), 149 (top)

Giraudi Wettstein, Architects, Lugano — 148 (bottom)

Rahman, Perween; Welfare Colony, in: Community Initiatives; ed. by Arif Hasan, City Press, Karachi, 1998 — 150

Planungsorganisation Stadtentwicklung; Testplanung Stadtmitte Winterthur, Departement Bau, Winterthur, 1992 — 152 (bottom), 153 (center)

Westermann, Reto; Neues Leben auf Industriebrachen, in: Forum 2, 2003, Bundesamt für Raumentwicklung, Berne, 2003 — 153 (bottom)

Burkard, Urs and Meyer, Adrian; DVZ Theaterstraße in Winterthur, in: Schweizer Ingenieur und Architekt 31/32, 2000, Zurich — 154

Boesch, Hans and Hofer Paul; Flugbild der Schweizer Stadt, Kümmerly & Frey, Berne, 1963 — 158 (top)

Francesco Guardi exhibition; art 9, 93, Frankfurt — 161

Hochbaudepartement der Stadt Zürich; Kooperative Entwicklunsplanung Quartier Leutschenbach, Zurich, 1999 — 163 (left top, left center, left bottom, right top, right center)

Ambühl, Iso; Darf ein Haus wie ein Hund aussehen? SonntagsZeitung 7, 1993, Zurich — 164

Stadtbauamt Feldkirch, Feldkirch — 165 (top)

Chramosta, Walter, Fingerhuth, Carl and Peer, Johann; Sichtung 1, Stadt Feldkirch, 2000 — 165 (center, bottom)

Fingerhuth, Carl and Merk, Elisabeth; Qualität für die Stadt durch Dialog über die Stadt: das Instrument der Stadtbildkommission, Öffentlicher Raum und Stadtgestalt, Bundesamt für Bauwesen und Raumentwicklung, issue 1/2, 2003, Bonn — 280–283

Fingerhuth, Carl; Plötzlich alles anders, in: Der Standard, December 7, 2002, Vienna. Dezember 2002, Wien — 168, 169

National Geographic Magazine, Washington — 172, 178, 184 (bottom)

Schwarz, Jutta; Nachhaltige Entwicklung, Schweizer Ingenieur und Architekt, February 20, 1997 — 174 (top)

Museum der Kulturen, Das südwestliche Paradies des Padmasambhava, postcard, 2003 — 175 (top)

Eitel, E.J.; Feng Shui, Felicitas Hübner, Waldeck, 1983 — 175 (bottom)

Westfälisches Schulmuseum der Stadt Dortmund, Dortmund Rider-Waite-Tarotdeck, U.S. Games System, Stamford — 180 (top)

Weber, Urs; Sonne und Mond – auf der Suche nach Kelten-Visuren, Basler Zeitung, November 28, 1968, Basel — 180 (bottom)

D'Aujourhui, Rolf; Die Entwicklung Basels vom keltischen Oppidum zur hochmittelalterlichen Stadt, Archäologische Bodenforschung des Kantons Basel-Stadt, Basel, 1990 — 181 (top)

Bauval, Robert, Hancock, Graham; Keeper of Genesis, Arrow, London, 1997 — 182 (top, center)

Atkinson, R J C; Stonehenge, English Heritage, London, 1987 — 183 (center, bottom)

Pennick, Nigel; Die alte Wissenschaft der Geomantie, Trikon-dianus, Munich, 1982 — 185 (center)

Kostof, Spiro; Das Gesicht der Stadt, Neue Zürcher Zeitung, 1992 — 186 (top left)

Eaton, Ruth; Ideal Cities, Thames & Hudson, New York, 2001 — 186 (bottom)

Sennhauser, Hans Rudolf; Stadtgrenze und Stadtsaum, in: Stadt- und Landmauern; ed. by Brigitt Siegel, vdf Hochschulverlag at the ETH Zurich, Zurich, 1999 — 188 (top)

Lorzestadt Zug, Entwicklungsansätze für das westliche Stadtgebiet; Stadtbauamt Zug, 1998 — 191 (top)

Geissbühler, Dieter, Koch, Michael, Rotzler, Stefan; Archithese special issue, Stadt-Landschaft oder Landschafts-Stadt Schweiz, Zurich, 2000 — 191 (bottom)

Kaltenborn, Olaf; Magische Orte, Klartext, Essen, 2003 — 192 (bottom) Gebr. König, Cologne; postcard, 1982 — 194

Werkner, Patrick; Land Art USA, Prestel, Munich, 1992 — 195 (top)

Billeter, Erika; Mythos und Ritual in der Kunst der siebziger Jahre, Kunsthaus Zürich, Zurich 1981 — 195 (bottom)

Buckley Ebrey, Patricia; China, Campus, Frankfurt/Main, 1996 — 197

Brouwer, Petra; Mastering the City II, ed. by Koos Bosma and Helma Hellinga, NAI Publishers, Rotterdam, 1997 — 200

Bacon, Edmund N.; Stadtplanung, Artemis, Zurich, 1968 — 208 (center bottom)

For years now, I've been collecting images of the city and recording them on transparencies. Many of the illustrations used in this book are from my collection. I can no longer remember where all of them came from. Every effort was made to trace the copyright owners. I apologize for any omission that may have occured.

INDEX OF PLACES

ACKNOWLEDGEMENTS

The following people read and provided commentary on the first draft of this book: psychiatrist Danilo Clamer; professor of urban planning Werner Durth; city architect Franz Eberhard; agent Dieter Hagenbach; editor Martin Frischknecht; theologian Peter Lack; urban scientist Martina Nitzl; storyteller Lilith Picard; urban planner Iris Reuther; journalist René Schneider; professor of landscape architecture Hille von Seggern; and architect Karin von Wietersheim. Their contributions to the intensity and clarity of this book have been invaluable. Finally, I would like to thank my wonderful wife Maggie Tapert for her love and support during the creation of this book.

————

Francis Hodgskin, Alfred von Sick, and Hans Zwimpfer contributed to the cost of printing this book. I thank them warmly for their support.

A CIP catalogue record for this book is available from
the Library of Congress, Washington D.C., USA

Bibliographic information published by Die Deutsche
Bibliothek. Die Deutsche Bibliothek lists this publication in
the Deutsche Nationalbibliografie; detailed bibliographic
data is available in the Internet at http://dnb.ddb.de.

This book is also available in a German language edition
(ISBN 3-7643-6983-3).

© 2004 Birkhäuser – Publishers for Architecture,
P.O. Box 133, CH-4010 Basel, Switzerland
www.birkhauser.ch
Part of Springer Science + Business Media

Translation into English: Elizabeth Schwaiger, Toronto
Text editor: Sarah Gonser, New York

Printed on acid-free paper produced
from chlorine-free pulp. TCF ∞
Printed in Germany
ISBN 3-7643-6943-4

9 8 7 6 5 4 3 2 1